PIRENE'S FOUNTAIN

PIRENE'S FOUNTAIN

Senior Editor	Lark Vernon Timmons
Submissions and Review Editor	Elizabeth Nichols
Design & Layout Editor	Steve Asmussen
Associate Editors	Royce Hamel Linda E. Kim Paul Kim Kelly Cressio-Moeller
Web Editor	Katherine Herschler
Art Consultant	Tracy McQueen
Publisher & Managing Editor	Ami Kaye

Pirene's Fountain
Skin Deep

Volume 10, Issue 18

Pirene's Fountain: A Journal of Poetry
Volume 10, Issue 18
Copyright © 2017 Pirene's Fountain
Paperback ISSN 2331-1096

Layout, Book & Cover Design: Steven Asmussen
Copyediting: Elizabeth Nichols & Linda E. Kim
Cover Artist: Katherine Herschler

All rights reserved: except for the purpose of quoting brief passages for review, no part of this book may be reproduced or transmitted in any form or by any means, electronic or mechanical, including photocopying, recording, or by any information storage and retrieval system, without permission in writing from the publisher.

Glass Lyre Press, LLC
P.O. Box 2693
Glenview, IL 60025

www.GlassLyrePress.com

Contents

Poetry

Kelli Allen
 It's Only A Weapon When You Hold Your Breath   11
Maura Alia Badji
 Advice for the Newly Beautiful   12
 Confession, a semi-cento   14
Amy Barone
 Beauty Editor   15
Susan Berlin
 Non-Stop Scarlet   16
 Unbareable Heat   17
 Praise for the Corpse Flower   18
Jan Bottiglieri
 I Take My Cancer To See The *RoboCop* Reboot   20
Patricia Clark
 Pierced   21
Joan Colby
 No Skin Off My Nose   22
Beth Copeland
 Pretty is as Pretty   23
Krista Cox
 A Woman Has an Obligation   26
  To Keep her Legs Shaven
Ken Craft
 The Age of Narcissism   27
Ivan de Monbrison
 Two poems painted with light   28
Hannah Dellabella
 Melting Point   30

Lori Desrosiers
    about the body   31
Anthony DiMatteo
    Father Time   32
Timothy B. Dodd
    Jigsaw Man   33
Alexis Rhone Fancher
    Poem For The Girl Who Wanted To Stop Time   34
Marcene Gandolfo
    Hide   35
Gail Fishman Gerwin
    Amélie's Complaint   36
Timothy Green
    At the Playground   37
    George Bush Painting   38
Melinda B Hipple
    Focus   39
Lois P. Jones
    One   40
Allison Joseph
    Opticals   41
    Babble   43
    Now Not Later   45
Kateema Lee
    Venus De Milo in Georgetown, D.C.   46
Dennis Maloney
    Sections from "The Faces of Guan Yin"   48
John C. Mannone
    The First Time Ever I Saw Your Face   49
Megan Merchant
    How to Raise a Girl   50
    How to Take a Selfie   51
Amy Miller
    Dream of the Old Body   52
    I Know Young People Are Mocking Me   53
Pamela Miller
    Beauty at Sixty-Five   54
    Autobiography Written in Disappearing Ink   55

Hallie Moore
    Barbies   56
    From The Table in Back   58

Cameron Morse
    Strange Tale from a Chinese Studio   59

Dipika Mukherjee
    Solomon's Temple   60

James B. Nicola
    In Beauty   61

Cristina M.R. Norcross
    You Are Limitless   62
    Letting Go of the Shell   63

Simon Perchik
    Untitled   64

Connie Post
    Fade In   65
    Back Stage   67

Marcia J Pradzinski
    kitchen portrait   68

Sandra Rokoff-Lizut
    No More Rain   69

M.C. Rush
    Presented Without Comment   70

Don Share
    On Screaming Your Head Off   71

Susan Sheppard
    Snap Apple Night   72

Alison Stone
    Not Always Beauty   73

Melissa Studdard
    Family Tree   74
    For Baudelaire   75

J. Tarwood
    Jennifer Eve   76
    A Small Rocky Island   77

Susan Tepper
    Half-made   78

Maria Terrone
    Sonnet After the Fall   79

Caitlin Thomson
    You Gave Me Madness   80
Wren Tuatha
    Maybe a Metronome   81
Pamela Uschuk
    Dharma   82
Ann Wehrman
    Desire   83
Martin Willitts Jr.
    The Kazusa Province Sea Route   85
Jane Yolen
    Sneewittchen   86

Showcase

Timothy Green   89
Dipika Mukherjee   100
Don Share   111

Reviews

Ambushing Water by Danielle Hanson   131
Equilibrium by Tiana Clark   135
Forty Miles North of Nowhere   140
    by LeRoy N. Sorenson
Riding Thermals to Winter Grounds   145
    by Djelloul Marbrook
Suites for the Modern Dancer by Jill Khoury   148
What Are We Not For by Tommye Blount   153
The Wire Fence Holding Back the World   156
    by Martin Willitts Jr.
Woman in a Blue Robe by Yoko Danno   160

Publication Credits
Contributor Notes

POETRY

It's Only A Weapon When You Hold Your Breath

Kelli Allen

In the body, there is a better reason.
The belly, and the faithful spleen,
as if breathing, suggests that you are on fire,
in flames, the orange burning brighter
the longer you stay on your knees.

You could look up. You might show
the white flash of your throat, the way
it uncoils under the skin when you swallow.
This, too, means ash is not far behind.

What smolders changes the longer
you press your tongue to the tight roof
of that mouth, language unnecessary, coming
much later, in the rifle barrel night.

So, are you praying now, in that field
all concrete spidered weeds and week-
old daylight? There it is, that split between
kneeling and exile, middling the city's
open jaws and your own. It is easier to answer
with your head tilted back, lashes wet and black.

Advice for the Newly Beautiful

Maura Alia Badji

You won't notice the change at first,
the way people look at you, not
through you. As though studying
the cover of a promising book.

You will walk down the street
in your old skin, imagining
you are your old self. Yet
slow changes are in place.

One day clothes won't fit,
will sag, your pants balloon
at ass and ankle. You have shed
your outer skin.

You are beautiful. You are thin,
that elusive goal you toiled
behind for decades is suddenly
yours, magically here.

You find the change in men's
eyes and women's: both
interest and threat, where once was nothing
so vague as a pause, a turning away.

In stores, the pretty clerk is cheerful,
snaps to attention when you request
smaller sizes. Sometimes
you announce the exact poundage

you have dropped, like a load of stones.
In celebration your mother
offers to buy you a new white
dress, weeps when it fits you perfectly.

To your surprise, you find you
miss Her: that other rejected you,
shadow-self, whose strong features once
diluted with fat and years of layered hiding

now shine. You sense
she's in there somewhere
waiting, loving your new
 plumage, but starving to death.

Confession, a semi-cento

Maura Alia Badji

I will begin with the body.
I got the armor, and the shine of a snake.

I keep it clean, oiled and some nights it seems
I live in an age of bodies delivering themselves to heaven.

I don't want to hurt a man, but I like to hear one beg. There is
A prayer that goes: Lord I am powerless…

Words that only begin to say what seethes. Give me the perfect
Circle of your voice. Cries and rough

Whispers over the traffic's sleek susurrus.
I want to rise onto your lips, linger

Like music in your throat, vanish
Like water under heat.
I will begin and return to the body
I wear your kiss like a stain.

I wait in the sugar cane fields,
Immortal and skin.

Sources: Maura Alia Badji, Roger Bonair-Agard, Jericho Brown, Missy Elliot, Terrance Hayes, Lynda Hull, and Parneshia Jones.

Beauty Editor

Amy Barone

Dream Maker:
I work in a field that triggers hope and renewal.
Every week fashion houses send the newest perfumes.
Intoxicating and infuriating scents fill the air.
Paris, New York, Tokyo, Milan.

Trail Blazer:
The new "it" accessory,
beauty replaced tired shoes and faddish bags.
I discover that cellulite creams really work.
Chanel, Bulgari, Coty, Dior.

Glamour Critic:
I visit perfumeries and analyze fragrances.
L'Oreal Paris won't take my calls.
I retort the customer knows all —
need the right message, wrap, ad, stores.

Researcher Extraordinaire:
My world covers science, culture, business, art.
Modern textures promise quick lifts.
Swirls of color hold the power to transform
looks, moods, demeanor, pose.

Miracle Worker:
The doubters see snake oil, believers take faith
in the exotic scent or perfect shade of red.
Friends hound me for industry secrets:
forsake sun and cigarettes, OD on water and sleep, smile.

Non-Stop Scarlet

Susan Berlin

Sounds less like a plant than a popular harlot,

but for nine bucks I take home from Maloney's Nursery this
Non-Stop Scarlet Tuberous Begonia whose red petals — ruffled
and raised as the Rockettes' skirts — display themselves
in frothy layers atop their hairy stems.

Ten days later, after wind has swept away the sapped blooms,
a new, improved version appears — less dense, the petals no longer
ruffled but smooth, the center of each flower pure yellow now
as if, overnight, filled with light.

How did Scarlet re-invent herself so soon? How quickly
she's raced through the slow-paced stages of my life,
catching up in no time to decades spent in search of
my self: deciding to shed her more frivolous frills
and build, instead, on what's at the core.

Unbareable Heat

Susan Berlin

Three days without power in triple digit heat
drives half the town to this cobblestoned corner
where the ice cream shop and coffee bar
meet. Two abreast, the line stretches
half way down the street.

I undo two, then three of the buttons
on my long sleeved linen shirt, hesitate to roll up
the sleeves, knowing the wrinkles may
never come out. I'm debating whether to fold up
the cuffs of my thick (but slenderizing) black pants when I notice
the woman standing next to me.

More ancient than old, she sports a pair
of very short shorts and a drooping halter top.
From both knees and thighs, richly varicosed
folds of skin drape like bunting
from firehouse windows.

My first thought — which I hate to admit — is:
Kill me if I ever look like that. Which yields, before
my next breath, to a hot flush of shame and then
an overwhelming sense of envy -- for her
defiance of fashion tips for women over 90,
her vanity-be-damned vote for comfort
over personal conceit. Just then

The woman leans toward me to offer a stick of gum and says:
*Poor thing — look at you, all bundled up. You must've come
from someplace cold.*

Praise for the Corpse Flower

Susan Berlin

Bless the *Amorphophallus Titanum* with its one colossal shoot,
    the ten-foot tall 'corpse flower' whose horrid smell
    mimics the rotting carrion above which it blooms.

Should we not praise the flower, despite its perfume?

Some applause, then, for the rabid dog, the lapsed priest,
    the unconvicted guilty, freed on their own recognizance.

Let's extol the barker, the telemarketer, the bigot, the boil,
    the swollen splinter dug deep, reddening your thumb.

One cheer each for the atheist and agnostic, for the scientist
    studying lunar rocks – ungodly hours, at 100 watts – and

how about the leagues of blue-haired thieves
    whose purses bulge with sugar packets, napkins, salt?

Kudos for recidivists like the roach and the self-obsessed talk show host.

Salvos for the pervert, the pimp, the ambition-driven centerfold.

A little hymn, too, for the also-rans: the torn ligament, the ruptured
    spleen, the dented can.

No confetti for the wet match, the little toe, the perpetually lesser than?
I say,

praise every crumb that falls, forever lost between cushions
   of the couch. Recognize the spent life. The long haul. Acclaim
   both sides of the hyphenated wife (battered- and -beater both),
   all jack-knifed, flailing, into the same free fall.

Praise the least of us, praise us all.

I Take My Cancer To See The *RoboCop* Reboot

Jan Bottiglieri

And in the dark I let her, eyeless, peek
through my eyes. My cancer is the secret
no one sees, curled above heart, beneath skin,
a new patriotism. We have popcorn,

we contemplate the body of a cop
who was exploded, now mostly machine:
his tender lungs under glass, their meat sheen;
his disassemble, whir and clank and flat

blank face. This movie is terrible, death
and not death both are terrible, there are
too many villains, my husband says.
Human: What the ones living in the near

future want. Consciousness, the override.
Nature: what sticks, invisible, inside.

Pierced

Patricia Clark

Janice was my friend, junior high,
who lived in a rental house. Another

friend warned me—there's something
wrong with that place.
And maybe her, too.

When she moved away, there was no goodbye.

My brother Michael was a baby then.
The Sound of Music was all the rage.
We danced with him

singing, "High on the hill was a lonely
goatherd." None of us could yodel.

Before my friend moved, she pierced

my ears with darning needles, after
I held two ice cubes to the lobes.

The holes are still there—
I touch them every day.

No Skin Off My Nose

Joan Colby

Taut, shiny, ominous bumps.
Small dangerous foothills
Where the bad dwarves dwell.
Pathology tells a story unfit
For the children of benevolence.
One of scalpels and frozen
Sections magnified and sliced,
A bloody pit enclosed with
Sutures, flaps or grafts.
Be heedless as the lingo. The shrug
Of a prisoner who gives nothing
But serial number and unit. Love
Tells no secrets, turns its back
To persuasion. The cells
Of misadventure thicken
In invasive clumps like
Purple loosestrife. Kill
Beauty to save the body.
That's the mission. The mind
Raves in its oozing cloak.

Pretty is as Pretty

Beth Copeland

Does. The doctor says, *You must*
have been beautiful when you

were young. Mother
struggles to lift

her head, hair mussed in a titmouse
tuft from the pillow, her cheeks—once milky

as magnolia petals—speckled
with age, but the wide-set

brown eyes and high cheekbones
people compared to Jackie

*****

Kennedy's still shine through.
At ten, I paused before

the mirror, removed my cat's
eye glasses, astigmatism

softening angles, round
cheeks rosy from pedaling

my Schwinn against
the wind, sprigs of hair

like sun spokes sprung
from my ponytail's elastic

band, eyes a blur of sage
ringed with smoke. Mama

fried okra while Becky scribbled
in a Sleeping Beauty coloring book

and baby Luke crawled
after a tennis ball. *Mama, am I*

pretty? She flipped a cornmeal
crusted pod with a fork. *You'll never*

be a great beauty. Crisco sizzled
and spat in the skillet. *But you're pleasing*

enough. My fantasy
of strutting down a runway

with an armful of long-stemmed
roses as Bert crooned, *There*

she is—Miss
America, shattered like a Coke

bottle on concrete. I checked
the mirror again, this time

in my glasses—I was plain,
with Daddy's aquiline

nose and pinched
lips, with darkening

hair she called *dishwater*
blonde. A good Christian

woman wasn't supposed to think
too highly of herself or—God

forbid—be vain. I was supposed
to be modest like Mama or brave

like Lottie Moon, the missionary
who starved to save Chinese children

*****

 for Jesus. Now I smooth
her unbrushed hair, so

sparse you can see her scalp. Yes,
I tell the clipboard

clutching doctor, my eyes locked
on his. *My mother was. She still is.*

A Woman Has an Obligation To Keep her Legs Shaven

Krista Cox

Adam, I will hide
your razors
until I can swing
from your face—
a choice vine, a completely faithful
seed. You were sculpted
from dust
to please me, to apple
my eye. Your body
is my temple
and I will throw my die
against your walls,
I will carve you
into shelves
for my collection
of feminist figurehead
dolls—Gloria Steinem
on your collarbone,
Roxane Gay in the scoop
of your pelvis, bell hooks
hooked above your missing
rib. Fair is fair
and you've always called us
the fairer sex, smooth
as prophetic illusion, cold
and pale for lack
of fleece.

The Age of Narcissism

Ken Craft

I read it in *The New York Times:*
We live in the Age of Narcissism.
To commemorate, *Bon Appetit* issues
its "culture" issue.
Nothing to do with Ancient Greece
or the Renaissance. Nothing to do
with the tang of sourdough starter
or tentacles of kombucha mothers.
People, rather. Photographing
their food before they eat it. Because
if it isn't uploaded
and shared, they didn't eat it.

From memory's rib, photography.
And after dessert, selfies. Where diners
hold the Palm God on high, stare down his shallow
pool. Sacrifice bulging eye-white, toothed hyperbole,
melon-slice smile.
Homily of click.
Benediction of send.

Check back for likes.
And more moments later. These are the new
immutables: the kiss of reaffirmation
and cold food.

Two poems painted with light

Ivan de Monbrison

le toit s'incline
un trou dans la lumière
et le miroir descend
on pleure
  la nuit s'étend
une dernière étoile tourne dans la lumière
la fenêtre fermée enferme le paysage
avec tout le sang dans tes yeux
le monde peint en rouge
à la forme de ton visage
les rêves s'allument un à un
dans le petit miroir
   mais plus loin dans la rue
une silhouette a glissé et tombe
dans la nuit
    c'est ton éclat de rire
       qui l'a fait déraper

      sous la tente
on pleure
quelque chose te dévisage
 la porte penche
une tête surgit
  les arbres sont toujours verts
le monde plus petit
on regarde la lampe
brûler en plein jour
  sous les mains de la pluie
      l'horizon s'est éteint
 et celui qui s'en va
  emporte une larme
     dans ses mains
un éclat de soupir
mais il reste trop humain pour ne pas en mourir
à l'horizon lointain

the tilting roof
a hole in light
and the mirror goes down
we cry
    the night stretches out
one last star is turning within light
the window closed encloses the landscape
with all this blood in your eyes
the world painted in red
has the shape of your face
dreams light up one after the other
inside the small mirror
      but way out on the street
a figure slipped and fell
into the night
    it is your laughter
        which caused it to fall down

    under the tent
someone is crying
something is staring at you
  the door tilting
a head pops up
    the trees are still green
the world is smaller
we look at the lamp
burning in full daylight
    under the hands of the rain
        the horizon turned off
and the one who's leaving
    holds a tear
        in his hands
the bursting of a sigh
which is far too human in order not to die
on this far horizon

Melting Point

Hannah Dellabella

I spent six months
plucking at wires
growing barbed from my veins.
They sprouted through my skin
like perverse blossoms, all thorn
and no rose. You held out
your hands to each metallic offering,
let me push someone else's poison
into you. I could see the way
it made you sick, the way you arranged
clenched teeth into a curve
that could be read as smiling.
I knew. I flickered with the idea
of holding all this metal myself.
I bent my wires. I reshaped
this body as if I could give it
a stronger form and tried
not to tremble. But I was a tuning fork
and everything was striking me.
You came to me then, steadied me,
hands warming everything
that had once been cold.
I had forgotten that metal could be molten,
that lips could draw poison from wounds.

about the body

Lori Desrosiers

how the house we carry with us changes,
what it feels like to see
the face age, how the breasts fall
how pain becomes a given
how the skin was once unblemished
and smooth, like the curve
of earth or sunbeams bent by trees
it is also about caves
the ones we dig to hide secrets
a wish to get beyond mirrors
how my mother is shrinking
she says she'll end up
a puddle in the kitchen
no one will recognize
this poem is about emerging
about finding beauty in imperfection
how skin stretches to accommodate
bones their restless march towards death.

Father Time

Anthony DiMatteo

That night I took a long, closer look.
I had more to learn then and still have.
Those two marbles tight in their little pink sac
would help bless two wives with a fine child,
girl and boy. Now one might test cancerous
and be removed before it spreads to its neighbor.
We prove guests of our body bound to its fate.
But back then, what did I know of love or loss?
My wisdom still makes the briefest of chapters.

Jigsaw Man

Timothy B. Dodd

The pieces lie scattered on the table, dumped
from the hollow cave, a cardboard god-box.
Bernard and Sasha can't stop pointing
at its illustration --- as if copying guides us
to completeness. A few fragments will fall
on the floor, in your lap, hide under others;
nothing seems significant in and of itself,
only in lieu of a hoped-for replica --- to finish
and get back to the mail, phone calls. Fun
only strange and vague sensations? To feel
those edges connect, join --- that's progress,
accomplishment. Followed by a hundred games

of solitaire? Jigsaw Man, were you purchased
at a Toys R Us --- in another strange and vague
plaza, car-cramped even off the highway? Only
more gasoline needed? Or are you, me, a corpse
in the bog, the incomplete, made from hundreds
of bodies, from different times and places never
seen, all merging together under the thick black
soupy night swamp until something forms ---
searching for a soul, rising up from the dank
to look at this mess, this puzzle spread so thin,
a web interlocked around us so tightly that we
can't sniff what's around the corner, our ancients
looking on, wondering if we'll put ourselves back
together --- a lonely death lying out on the table,
scraps someone chopped up, boxed up, and sold.

Poem For The Girl Who Wanted To Stop Time

Alexis Rhone Fancher

when the sirens made apartment dogs keen,
she howled for him - her body a longing

                                                                                              she gave away all her clothes
                                                                                              she knew no one could love her
                          because he danced solo
                          because she flew planes into mountains
                          because she circled the drain

her Scorpio was in Venus; he'd left his in a stranger's bed.
                                                                    she needed what was left of him
                                                                    it was an inside job

he wanted too much   he didn't come home
he couldn't choose   he hated silence
                                                                        he couldn't love

                          because she lived in the outfield
                          because he feared the dark
the trees were crying
                          she stumbled and fell
she couldn't take it
back
               before she knew it, the stars had misaligned
                       the moon was in Paris
                       the astrologer smelled of beer
she'd lie if questioned
she knew the ropes

she ate like a bird   the shoes pinched
the ocean waved   he left her stranded
the clock stopped   she wanted to die
he always left
she always forgave him

                                     now that he was dead
                                          and
                                that girl had disappeared.

Hide

Marcene Gandolfo

This house is a thick coat. A coat lined with silk. A skin that tickles. Some winters all I need is a heavy sweater. Some days my skin is made of first-grade paper mâché. Once I built an empty house from mom's Marlboro cartons. I painted it ecru and antique white. Those years what I needed was a windbreaker. When I lean against eggshell walls I don't know where my body ends and house begins. Once I built a roof of matchboxes. I painted it tickle-me-pink. Some days I go out in the cold without a coat, without a sweater. I wander away from my house so I can lose it: to remember I live in a theatre of skin.

Amélie's Complaint

Gail Fishman Gerwin

—After The Painter's Family, Matisse, 1911

Such color Henri, why did I let you clothe this room you have no concept of what melds yet that is what brings you fame, what pays our debts Our boys—why you attire them in red puzzles me—need to attend to schoolwork while they have light, examinations tomorrow, they're hungry, tired, why are they playing chess She sits, your daughter Marguerite, you place her in the background, high in the air though even a fool knows that a sofa couldn't remain in such a position She crochets, why am I not next to her I accepted her as my own, you paint her incessantly, that black neck ribbon to hide scars of diphtheria And these shoes you place on my feet, they point, they pinch, they're blue though I prefer black, at least you gave that to my dress The mantle you fix—like us—in two dimensions, is that how you see us, two dimensions, watch the vases fall to the floor, your naked sculpture ready to topple Hurry Henri, I am in the middle of a good book, the ragout ready to burn, this posing, endless posing, can't you let your imagination work for you and let us be Finish the work before we fall from the canvas, fold like bolts of fabric to the floor, your scarlets, golds, your incessant blues, blended like the arrangement we endure.

At the Playground

Timothy Green
for Elise

I can see the smart
of her eyes but
can't tell what
she's saying,
can't tell if
it's the missing
teeth or more.
Tough to talk
without those two
in particular—
tongue
sloshing through
gum with every
slurred word.
The soft quick
of it, though,
the shy concision,
as if each was
a stone stored
in her mouthful
of stones,
and the whole
of her speech
could spill.

George Bush Painting

Timothy Green

Somewhere in the desert a hungry dog tied to a rope wags its tail
each time the owner passes, knowing it won't be fed.
Somewhere in Texas, the former President, Bush the Younger,
finishes painting his 51st Yorkshire Terrier. What can be done
with these facts? Bush the Clown, Bush the Caricature, Bush
in a cowboy hat clearing brush, his work clothes artificially aged
for the cameras like forged art. Even his nickname is counterfeit—
not the folksy familiar "Dubya," but "W.," as in Walker,
a tribute to the family that his family has served. His father
was a goon, but a global goon, a good soldier in the war for wealth.
The Bay of Pigs Invasion (codename: Operation Zapata)
was staged off the island leased by his oilless oil company,
Zapata Offshore. The name of the boat that brought the rebels?
The Barbara J. And where were you when they killed JFK?
The Elder Bush was in Dallas, calling it Tyler for the paper
trail. These are facts, too, but don't get distracted.
We're here for the son who knows them, posing now
beside his portrait of a Corgi. LESSONS TOOK PLACE
AT UNDISCLOSED LOCATION reads the banner
at the bottom of the screen. Even his art teacher won't admit
to this pupil, and let's just say it: The paintings are awful.
The heads of the dogs don't fit their bodies. Their legs are tubes
of toilet paper, straight down to the paw, as they stand or sit
over shadows like puddles of oil. His other subjects are almost
as bad—a cat in a pot, a cross on a table, his feet at the end
of a tub. But the dogs are the worst, and so many of them—
over 50, each one expressionless, pleading vacant at the viewer—
each of them George himself, his seven minutes reading *The Pet Goat*.
Don't imagine the paintings, but imagine the man some called
Leader of the Free World, working on the curve of his own
big toe, over and over and never getting it right. Quick enough
to know that he's slow. Grown boy in the emperor's robes.
And standing beside these paintings on television,
his always-embarrassed grin, knowing what he knows,
hope and hopelessness drawn in equal measure.

Focus

Melinda B Hipple

Some days I want to unpack myself.
Unbutton my skin and drape it
over the back of a chair. No longer worry
about wrinkles. Stack my bones in the corner,
and set aside this packet of organs
that keep a body humming. I want to
step out of everything that is vulnerable.
Move through the world without
distraction. Discover a universal truth
not dependent on need or tempted by want
or driven by fear.

One

Lois P. Jones

One lifetime she drank water from his skull.
She gilded the bones with gold and struck them
in the dirt. She pounced a vowel that was her name.
But now she is no one. She has the privilege
of ambiguity. Being one white woman,
being from nowhere but earth
and a father who lost his mind
in the metal.

Being this way, she is; an American
indistinguishable as a flesh tree
in the desert. She wishes for a name
like Kandinsky, Levertov. How about Stradivarius?
How about dinner on the 41st floor? She did arrange this.
She did write the composer a letter.

Meet me on the roof of One Wilshire.

She brought wine and a white summer
dress. She brought nothing underneath
but the long boulevard of empty offices
lit up like an afterthought. The cot
she carried up 11 flights of stairs. She brought
the night, slippery as a man on wheels.
She wheeled the stars until they were all
in their right places. She gave him all
the words an evening has for loneliness.

Opticals

Allison Joseph

Without them I stumble to see, two fogged
windowpanes over my lids, hooks on each end
to latch them over my ears, tiny translucent pads
that sit on the bridge of my nose, the whole contraption
held together by screws so tiny I couldn't see them
if they fell to the floor, lodged in the carpet.
"Made in Japan" is printed on one earpiece
in white lettering so minute it looks as if the tiniest
brush in the world must have made the JAPAN.
So much more flexible than I am, and without them
everything looks worse: words blurry around edges,
but with them I can see my own flaws better, whether
or not I want to—these lenses make every pore
visible. They own their own house, case
that opens and shut with a click, protects them
while I sleep, keeping safe their skinny little hinges,
the wire frames around their smudged ovals,
my thumbprints manic all over their surfaces.

If I sat on them, they'd break. The woman's voice
on my cell phone says it's time to see
the eye doctor again. I ignore her and squint at
the fine print on my bills. One scratch and they
are useless. My husband takes them off my face
and swears, *how do you see out of these things?*
They grow oily from the touch of my fingers—
after years of declining eyesight I still check
to see if they are there. In sunlight, their lenses
turn black so my corneas don't get scorched,
so I look like a cop from a 70's TV show or an
alien with sockets for eyes. Note to self: avoid
sunlight. I'll wear them to the movies, but not in photos.

I finally found this pair that fits across the bridge
of my broad nose without those dastardly red

marks, but the right earpiece fits more snugly
which makes me think my ears are deformed,
or the optician had no idea was she was doing.
But I wear them, perched precarious and silly,
push them back onto my nose all day long.
At night, I slip them back into their smooth velvet house.
Night's the only time I don't need them
because I don't see anything in focus as I dream.

Babble

Allison Joseph

Some days I stumble into speech,
feel awkward as my stubborn tongue
betrays my brain with words
that feel alien as rain
set loose inside my fading mind.
I try to make it right,

stumble even more to make it right,
face flushed as I garble easy speech.
It's hard when my sleepy mind
can't keep up with my rapid tongue,
ideas as slippery as rain,
rush of all these constant words

making me hate the reality of words,
fearing I'll never get them right.
A poet, I should feel right as rain
with all the possibilities of speech,
should be proficient in my native tongue,
not so crazed about my feeble mind.

All would be better if I didn't mind—
didn't care so much about loving words,
unconcerned about my dumb tongue.
Who cares if I say every little thing right,
if I'm eloquent in every single speech,
music of my voice like so much rain?

Not everyone's a fan of rain.
Not everyone admires an adroit mind.
So many folks are terrified of speech;
so many folks aren't in love with words,
and don't care if some word is wrong or right.
As a schoolgirl, I went to therapy for my tongue

because teachers said I had a flawed tongue,
unable to say "th" sounds like soft rain.
They were so far from being right,
but those sessions still haunt my mind
and when I trip over my own words,
I remember being yelled at for my speech.

But what child's speech has settled yet on her tongue?
All I knew were words, desperate as rain.
In retrospect, in my mind's eye, I hear my voice. It's right.

Now Not Later

Allison Joseph

Don't wait until I'm dead to celebrate
my life, my words, the clever things I said,
my small indignities, my loves, my hates.
Don't weep for me; rejoice instead.

Recall the ways my appetite was fed:
strong wines, good sex, full plates
of pasta, all sauces, white and red.
Don't wait until I'm dead to celebrate

the days I walked this earth. Don't wait
until my sense of taste is dead,
those days when disability is fate.
My life, my words, the clever things I said—

relive them now, keep them inside your heads
to use when I'm disconsolate,
too tired to get out of bed.
My small indignities, my loves, my hates,

the qualities I don't appreciate,
remind me of it all. The life I've led
won't help me when it's grown too late.
Don't weep for me. Rejoice instead

when I am gone, no longer wed
to flesh and breath. Think of the date
I die, but not with tears or dread,
with joys that don't disintegrate.
Don't wait.

Venus De Milo in Georgetown, D.C.

Kateema Lee

*I learned the truth at seventeen, that love
was meant for beauty queens —Janis Ian*

At seventeen, I had the body
of a goddess; even the boys

who preferred light skinned girls
wanted me, wanted to place

their hands on hips sculpted
by gods, caress the curves

of my C cups. At times,
I thought I was beautiful;

the "hey shorty" calls from cars,
the guys on the A bus asking

to walk with me, singing
"come and talk to me,"

an anthem for girls who never believed
they were beautiful until that song.

In Georgetown on M street,
my friends and I would walk

the block to Georgetown Park mall,
stop traffic, hear shouts,

"come over here," be invited
into dayglo clubs despite our age.
We were women swaying
to honked horns and sinister smiles—

we knew what they wanted,
we thought we knew what we wanted,

we didn't want the same things,
but we had our hips,

we still had our arms,
and for love we would give anything.

Sections from "The Faces of Guan Yin"

Dennis Maloney

Fragrant as a
scented oak
flowers in my hair
but with old age
it smells like damp
matted dog hair

My body a
palace of pleasure
now a dilapidated
house of pain
plaster sloughing off

....

Young and intoxicated
with my own lovely skin,
figure and gorgeous looks,
dressed to kill, despised
by other woman, I was
a hunter of fools

Today, head shaved,
wearing robes,
wandering for alms
I am myself with
no thought,
ties undone,
no men or goods,
I have quenched
those fires

The First Time Ever I Saw Your Face

John C. Mannone
After Roberta Flack

Smoke spirals above bar room crystal,
sweet bourbon & vermouth intoxicates
maraschino cherry, and orange, in the glass;
it wafts with midnight blues in a NY nightclub.
Her B-flats whisper, melancholy the theater
of my heart. It only quivers, feels applause
of bluesy piano keys; I sense only her lips'
gloss forming those perfect heart notes.

How to Raise a Girl

Megan Merchant

I read that calling her pretty
is the same
as slicing the vein up its blue line.

That I should say *smart,*
compliment her character,

her slanted-wit,

her knack for planting
and song, coloring in the lines,
not the bright of her eyes.

But we met only once.

At a party, where everyone was
masked and scrubbing their hands
for powered gloves.

The room was lit and cold,
but the drugs were good.

I never felt them climb inside,
tug her free, bless her with
staples of light.

I dreamt we were pulling opals
from a river of windows and bone,

her eyes, green as the lullaby
my grandmother would sing
to gauge

what the heart thinks it can
hold in the swollen-dark.

How to Take a Selfie

Megan Merchant

Take a match, burn away the sidelines of thighs until
there is a gap wide enough for an eye-slit to graze,

shave cheekbones to a point, needlepoint lips
until they swell and plump, gloss hair with seaweed

and motor oil until it shines, swallow tapeworms
so they can chew the fat while you thin.

Listen to the voices in your head that slap happiness
into wanting. While you sleep,

let moths chew little star-holes through your confidence.
Narcissus was a fool.

If you find yourself standing on the shore, throw stones
at the glimmer, recoil from the pixels of imperfection,

leave your image unworthy of love,
stranded, drowning.

Dream of the Old Body

Amy Miller

It came in like a ghost,
a languid cloud inhaled,
and sprang the bones and belly
from the burdens they had grown
themselves. Old as in

what was, as in
the dress that seemed like
nothing—just a pale sunset
from shoulder to the flat rock
of hip. The hands, too, forgot

their swollen calibrations
and the head—that window
with the frightened
pilot inside—was ready
for a climb or the sting

of some exotic insect, ready
to shower cold again
in a stone bunker at 6 a.m.,
unconcerned with the rattles
and spasms to come,

lost in the reedy call
of a bird outside the window
and the soft clothes
hanging on the door,
waiting to be filled and moved.

I Know Young People Are Mocking Me

Amy Miller

Can't wear those boots,
those pin-toes, cleat feet,
disharmonious clatter in the hall
and then up to that
small
skirt.

Whose knees
are knocking young men off
their pedestals?
Not these.

Knees,
thine are the speckled stockings
of '80s misfit dancing,
lock-kneed clamp
with a college girl
under the table
at Upstart Crow Café.

And now it's only *purse*.
As in *disapproving lips*.
As in *silk*. As in *sow*.
Small swing
on a long conservative
strap. Pockets,
dig in
for a lean winter.
Remember the singing
of coins
playing
in the deep.

Beauty at Sixty-Five

Pamela Miller

Cento from Anne Sexton

Once I was beautiful. Now I am myself
as I spill toward the stars in the empty years
with a singing in the head,
mouths calling mine, mine, mine.
Women are born twice.
I am beating all my wings.
I'm all one skin like a fish,
secretly naming each elegant sea.
A thousand doors ago
I thought I'd die — but here I am,
neither abstract nor pale,
a woman of some virtue and wild breasts.
Although I will inherit darkness,
good news, good news:
In celebration of the woman I am,
I soar in hostile air,
citizen and boss of my own body still,
so full of its immediate fever.

Autobiography Written in Disappearing Ink

Pamela Miller

Nobody ever called me Little Miss Whomp-Bam-Boom
or Flamethrowin' Fifi or

anything, really. At school I was voted
Most Likely to Evaporate.

I seemed to be cloistered in a convent of skin.
I was colorless and quiet as a mollusk.

At thirty I got married
to a room full of dimly lit mist.

In the world's grand bouquet, I was a budbound rose
that blooms every fifty million years.

I wanted my life to be an opera, a conflagration,
not this tiny threadbare prayer mouthed by mutes.

When I die, I'll carve *Remember Me*
on a tombstone made of vanishing breath.

Barbies

Hallie Moore
after Anne Sexton

With bodies nothing is forever.
Bodies are faultlines and earthquakes
that roll, then unroll,
go slack —all is flux .

boobs, butt, belly, the brain
all go to flab.

Little girls grow valleys and mountains.
        Men move continents to reach them.
Older, they swell in and out like sails,
        All is natural.
                  Flesh and bone.

As I write this sentence our bodies are eroding,
more bodies growing up.
        It's an assembly line with no off-switch,
           multiplying mirrors in nature's fun house.

Even after fifty-six millennia
since leafy Eden, nothing has changed
        (well maybe Botox and Juvaderm)
humans still molder
               and pass on.
 Yet,
we act like Malibu Barbie
looking for the next trend.
Live in our glass beach houses
        and if The End should come in the form of The Big One
           to rattle our sea view sending us down into the wet,
we fashion dolls wouldn't know how to swim.
 For all you who are fading
and there are many who will be shocked when they look in the mirror,
        many whose bodies will never be features in People
magazine—

                    even on your best days,
for those with body-illusions I say
            tenderly,
take off your designer bikinis,
your Jimmy Choo shoes, your diamond nose studs,
then unscrew your tanned arms and legs,
unroot the bleached hair from your head.
            Get down to the beating heart.

From The Table in Back

Hallie Moore

—on meeting expressionist artist Fulker

See a squint of sadness in these women looking at me:
a gray pocked tree, limbs crooked and leafless,
no longer the young bull who made them giggle
in fear when I unwrapped this gift of body.

My boots strode into yellow rye fields,
their ripe seed heads bent to my step, then
after the day's sweat, striding into meadows
of lush women, I knew their heads too would bend
to my body's promise.

Those spring days
my muscled arms grabbed the sun
and squeezed until pure art oozed from my pores.
I lacked sense to call it joy. I believed the dance
and the dancer would never end.

Here, let me offer you a beer.

Strange Tale from a Chinese Studio

Cameron Morse

At the ghost station, sliding doors sigh. Red lanterns billow like jellyfish above an empty platform. You board and sit down beside me, silkworms spinning moonlight into your cheongsam. Our arms close into a single seam. I know you're uncomfortable. I know it itches. You only wear your human skin for my benefit. A map of the Beijing subway system wriggles its 18 tentacles upon the wall. The last train of the night trundles into the dark—not of the tunnel, nor the stars, but your black hair. Every night we play the same game. Every night we get off at the same stop and you follow me home. I've been married to you my entire life without ever knowing your name.

Solomon's Temple

Dipika Mukherjee

On Leiden's streets, this is easy to miss
a tiny white building so nondescript,
so drab, so dull, it would not be remiss
to pass by without thought of manuscripts.

Seven centuries old, it knows of books
silk-wrapped, hand-inked on skin by silent scribes,
over cobblestones brought on padded hooves,
past dark canals, by horsemen greased with bribes.

What horde of treasure, hidden heresy
resided among Calvinists? Pages
worth more than gold, a promised ecstasy
of forbidden new thought, brave new ages?

A bookstore now, like many on that road,
the window flaunts stacks of Da Vinci Code.

Note: In the 14th century Philip of Leiden, Canon of St. Pancras, stipulated in his will (1372) that his book collection should remain intact in his house in Pieterskerkhof, so that his books could be loaned on guaranty. This house became popularly known as "Solomon's Temple" and is now a thriving bookstore in Leiden, Netherlands.

In Beauty

James B. Nicola

after Byron

They work in beauty through the night,
he, crazed with scraggly flaxen hair,
she, toothless and a sorry sight:
but neither of them seems to care.
And in their eyes I catch a light
that makes their aspects thrilling there.

I'd never heard of such a man
or woman who would rather sue
the white and mighty Ku Klux Klan
or heal the poor and birth a new
babe in some place like Pakistan
than follow interests we pursue.

And while one race remains in need
of legal wisdom and finesse,
while there is yet one mouth to feed
that bone and sinew might ache less,
there Beauty goes to sweat and bleed
in unbecoming humbleness.

Mother Teresa, 1910-1997
Morris Dees, b. 1936

You Are Limitless

Cristina M.R. Norcross

There is beauty in broken places –
the parts we cling to –
the memories kept hidden
in crevices kept close.

Where Light escapes and shines,
awareness lays bare our truths.
It begins to heal
what remains hidden.

We break open.
We uncover the soft underbelly
of vulnerability –
the tender heart.

Who calls to you,
when the shadows come?
Who dwells behind the door
that is you?
The inner voice who says,
you are loved.
You are safe.
You are limitless.
This is the one, true voice.
Listen to this
above all others.

There is beauty in broken places.
There is strength in the deepest canyon.
There is beauty in every, sacred facet
that is you.

Letting Go of the Shell

Cristina M.R. Norcross

This is the story of an egg shell –
the thin sheen of white
separating the vulnerable now
from the certainty of tomorrow.

I am not this, says Perfection.
I am not enough, whispers Insecurity.

Cactus-like isolation –
the sharp paralysis of standing still –
we are unable to hear
even the closest plane flying overhead.

A milky, gauze veil falls,
when we allow light
to permeate all things.
With eagle-eyed vision,
we see the beauty of a broken branch
with the same reverence
as beach plum petals about to bloom.

So this is how we break.
So this is how we mend.

Untitled

Simon Perchik

You button this sleeve the way smoke
is trained —a sudden shrug
and the night moves under you

can't see you're still on your feet
and though they no longer fit
the ground is already a crater

where her shadow would have been
holding on from behind
as a clear, moonlit dress

and the last thing you saw left open
as the slow, climbing turn
that's still not over.

Fade In

Connie Post

In a room far off from the main hallway
In front of the mirror
each actor places a painted mask
over their face

They have spent years
with oil based stains
leaking down the backs of their necks

Each paper Mache curve
was molded by the hands of a sinner
painted by the sacrament of deep red

they know how to breathe
inside the mask
how to measure the air of atonement

they know their voices sound muffled
when the audience leans forward
and pretends to understand the rehearsed lines

they understand that death
is an understudy

they think that each time they
enter and exit my dreams
that I won't recognize them

but I stand off stage
unseen, not breathing
watching how they sneak
into these perverse scripts
the man who does the lighting
always paralyzed

following the skirted line of velvet robes

each curtain a silence

Back Stage

Connie Post

You are like a stripper
who never takes off her clothes

you speak as if
you have spent your life on stage
but stay fully clothed
behind a dark curtain

on occasion
you perform a tangled dance
barely lift your skirt to onlookers
they never see
your thin shoulder blades
your rib cage that rises and falls
with each breath

you hold your thoughts
like worn dollar bills
dirty – and close to the hip

your scarves
are folded carefully
with the rest of your memories
in a mahogany dresser drawer
always off its track

you don't tell anyone
why you sleep in your clothes
why you fold yourself in two places
before bed

how the night enters you

your whole body a fugue

kitten portrait

Marcia J Pradzinski

my mother's hands
powder the wheat-hued
breadboard and smooth
flour evenly.

her wedding band
a part of her body
glints gold
on the puffy flesh
of her ring finger.

she rests the dough ball
on her palm and
rolls it from right
hand to left as her fingers
pat its round bloom

the dough something
she can prompt
with a tender whisper
into the shape
she fashions.

her floured arms lean
into the compliant mass
palms massaging
its growth.

snowy dots freckle
her arms and she pushes
hard as the windows
darken around her.

No More Rain

Sandra Rokoff-Lizut

Her yellow watering can
ends the thirsty roots'
silent screams.

A newly revived poppy
arches its thin neck
and smiles,

as three yellow tears
drip, drip, drip
into the watering can.

Presented Without Comment

M.C. Rush

Those who insist there is beauty only in filth
are as silly as those who see it only in purity:
beauty, like god, is everywhere
and nowhere.

Things exist in order that the difference between them might exist.
This space, this separation of definitions, is the blossoming of creation
to which the edges are only punctuation.

Looking at a volume of water,
how much can we care, really,
that it was once a large number of snowflakes,
no two the same?

On Screaming Your Head Off

Don Share

The voices of my world were not tender and unquestioning
—*W. S. Di Piero*

Drink your ass off, scream your head off! It's why
God gave you that molecule of his indecipherable wrath.
When you calm down again, talk to me. Sorry,
I have to go where my skin goes, an empath
out of sympathy for himself who has to overcome
this shitty cold to go Easter egg hunting, lordy me.
The letter I would write to my daughter is not
the letter I would write to my wife. "Dear Wife,"
I'd say, "When you calm down again, talk to me."
I've stopped getting haircuts, I wear muddy shoes
and rumpled clothes, sport a fresh chip on my shoulder.
But the worst thing is...not wanting to fly:
of all impossible things, the most impossible.
I turn up hopelessly late – at airports, at parties,
for work, and frankly, I'm better late than never.
When you calm down again, talk to me, OK?
Wild anything, fishy screamer, I'll tell you a tale
of the Yo-Semite I yam, of my pyrrhic experience as a seer.
I'm...a slow learner... entirely self-taught. I lie.
I'm a glaciologist of gloom, which is as bad as it sounds
so cue the engrams! Send in the clowns!
We had a love-hate relationship on a sinking ship.
But I'm ready to settle in a library of hills, I'm willing
to drink sequoia wine, guzzle sequoia blood
among squirrels, happy to write my woody gospel.
When you calm down again, remember wordy me.

Snap Apple Night

Susan Sheppard

I fall asleep to the briar songs of witches,
Those who circle me with miniature bells
Attached to thorn fingers, the ones
That unflesh the golden fruit that falls
On some black, unholy ground,
Left to simmer and swarm
Like other brooding souls.
Among the bearded hags of trees,
I turn these stones into conjurer's bones
Let them to rattle in my pockets.
I know this darkness will cause
My cells to open like ghost flowers,
As my body hums alone on its bed
And my skeleton rises from its sleep
To walk down a lonely road.

Not Always Beauty

Alison Stone

Some truths please the mouth
with sweetness, tangy
pucker, or salty crunch.
Facts to be savored.
Others I choke back
like this virus
with its stench of blood
and back-alleys, its magic trick
of making friends disappear.
Indelible as a rap sheet,
vengeful as a mirror.
Thirty-year dark cloud.
Secret of my sallow skin
and cancellations.
Dry bone always
splintering in the throat.

Family Tree

Melissa Studdard

My mother was a lake
        full of water lilies,

my father was a bridge
        between the bardo

and heaven. He tossed me
        to his shoulders for

the parade of grandparents
        at night: Orion and

Cassiopeia, Gemini and Auriga.
        Once we saw a cousin

shoot from the ground beside
        a circle of pines. *Geyser,*

Mother said, tossing a silver
        carp into the air. When

I was old enough, I asked them
        the story of my birth, and

they each handed me a singing
        sparrow the color of my hair.

For Baudelaire

Melissa Studdard

In the woods you found a carcass with maggots in its chest,
with waterfalls in its eyes, with the buzz of life still

hovering around its skull, and in commemoration, you grabbed
your sweetheart's hand, with your left, and on your right, you

snatched the clasped hand of the world and said: Look here, how
we build skyscrapers in the cavity of death's groin, how we

paint lilacs on its ribs. We will drive motor cars over its
bones and laugh in the waning perfume of midnight, and, my love,

I will write you a poem, a tribute to your beautiful decay,
to your rotting thighs, to the death you will birth with sex

because, truly, this is beauty—this festering carcass in the woods,
this putrid nag, truth. And in it, you will live forever.

Jennifer Eve

J. Tarwood

Girl child would sweep
a beach towel over her head
to parade like a freed Rapunzel.
Length's her promise kept
to the little one she used
to be, measuring her golden cape
growing far in mirrors.
Often now the mistress
of her scalp frustrates
like a friend certain
of attention however
many needs might needle.
Has hair become a cult
of brushes and barrettes,
shampoos and sinks?
A curing cut and she'd be
liberated like the lonely,
past pulverized, showers quick.
She combs out knots
threatening to cyclone,
thinking one word
still spoken, still unbroken.

A Small Rocky Island

J. Tarwood
(After Rossetti)

If somebody knows how
to excuse my straying,
to explain the nonsense
of my blood, I implore:

before the jasmine of my womb
dies, my moons punctual,
robustly complete, and my veins
exhaust themselves, so many
twilights, thighs scraping
thighs, knowing ivory, thinking
fire: before age demands
from my meat and bones
all vehemence, please

tell me.

Contemplate the mirror lodged
in my savannah, fertilely signaling
an inclement night. There
smooth linen pours, there
the hard flint of a guy
binding as a belt. Quicksilver
scrutiny. Strawberries below
my blouse. Anxious, stiffening
skin. My leaning back. A caress,
apparently;
and my mouth glows.

If somebody knows how
to excuse my wilding heart,
to deliver the fury my passion stipulates,
I beseech, before I smother
off my own fragrance, please,
please, I pray:

have a drink with me.

Half-made

Susan Tepper

Her skin, once redolent, has been reduced
to a simple thread pulling across bone
and ligaments 'til it resembles nubby cloth.
Browning, decayed. Gently rubbing lotion
I try and lubricate her loose dry flesh
from which I was half-made.
She wants no part of it. She wants
to be exactly the same as before
though she can't articulate this desire.
A smart woman she knows her body
is under siege. We see that in her,
my sister and I, grieving through all
the small moments time turns into debris.

Sonnet After the Fall

Maria Terrone

Every skin pierce a possible intrusion,
every itch the signal of disease—
and so our lakeside idyll becomes the unease
that returns all my old suspicions.
This peace, this beauty are the illusions
of a fool. Our friends who'd visited here just called
from Emergency Care, three ticks burrowed
under their skin. Who knows where the deed was done?
Threats lie everywhere, unseen, even in my breast
as I learned nine years ago, symptomless. As my friend,
a poet and musician knew, who succumbed
at fifty-six a month ago, her music arrested
mid-song. As the carp we watched knew too late,
flapping in a raptor's claw sideways, as if on a plate.

You Gave Me Madness

Caitlin Thomson

A longing to unzip my skin like a selkie
and climb into yours. You do not seem to long

for anything. There is satisfaction for you
in the order of days. My skin can stay mine,

you seem to say with your arm. Mouth
silent, yawning. Nothing tender

in the morning, dark with winter.
There is silence in the way your lips meet

the mug, the heel of bread, the egg.
Brilliant yoke against your skin.

Maybe a Metronome

Wren Tuatha

The work is done, anyway.
You dragged me out of my cave, just by your scent,
and the you I attached to it.

And so I lost weight,
remembered I had hair and styled it.
I bought clothes in case you might
notice. You might have.

I studied your movements, as if you were a
constellation I would join in the velvet blanket, as if
you were a timepiece, maybe a metronome,
and you would hear me sing and chord.

You might have, but you couldn't admit it.
You had momentum, you had flow.
You had a passport and I had a cave.

So I am alone still but the work is done.
Some other lonely hunter will swirl around
the kill you missed in your momentum,

the corazon you crushed in your flow.

Dharma

Pamela Uschuk
for Marnie Hillsley

Blue sky breathes through hummingbird's throat.
Who made the moat where red ants and Harris Hawk dream?
My fingers lace clouds into a shawl
of thunder and wind. I think of a friend,
whose face I've never touched, how
to memorize all the colors of her eyes,
how ever to sing for her the way
eagle feathers catch the sure intent of stars.
Ah, to wake in the desert, creosote-heady with last night's rain,
breeze cool as glass fingering palo verde's
buttery blooms, a collared lizard
in iridescent armor creeping from the Spanish Sword, five
baby quails noodling to strewn seed.
I can almost touch the calliope hummingbird
who mines orange trumpet flowers
reaching beyond itself
with its thin black tongue.
We feed a long line of hungry ghosts.
Changing shape a thousand times a morning, clouds
never stop loving wind
that pushes them over the horizon's brink.
The heart is memory's toughest muscle.
Break the mirror. Never forget
one lovely jagged piece.

Desire

Ann Wehrman

I finally bought
an electric-blue, Speedo one-piece
at Ross—$9, size 16.
Confronting myself in my bathroom mirror,
sweat blending with nervous chills,
I tug the damn thing on—
it rolls and clings,
too tight for my size-18, middle-aged body.
Armed with apartment keys, SPF, and a hair tie
I brave the glowing turquoise pool.

Too old, too shy, too many years alone,
too long since high school summers
when we swam every day at Sheridan,
deep Coppertone tans
Friday night dances on the patio
above the pools, under the stars.

Dip my toes, slip into the blue.
I kick, push, glide
through cool water,
surface and blow,
laze on my back, blinded
by white sunlight
stretch though some laps.

The gate clangs,
in stroll teen goddesses, lithe, lovely
their young men bantering—
the pitch rises.

I paddle to the side, mood shattered
re-wrap my cellulite in severity
climb the stairs at the shallow end
reclaim my flip-flops
re-key my door.

The Kazusa Province Sea Route

Martin Willitts Jr.

Haibun
Based on the painting #20 from Thirty-Six Views of Mount Fuji, by Katsushika Hokusai

What is beauty? Is it two junks carrying unknown treasures in treacherous water and finally discovering the calm? Nature is seen and not seen. What do you see in the noiseless sea spray or the sails full of helpful wind? Do you see the lives of the trees that were sacrificed to build the ships? I see the beauty in the unfamiliar.

I greeted my wife every day, *how I wish you would be mine.* I trace the tiny lines of connecting skin, cross-hatching and holding together what is true and believable. Now I am rocking inside a boat instead of in the arms of my lover. How familiar is the unfamiliar? No matter how often I scanned every inch of her, I never seem to notice every detail. There were so many details and so little time in life. So why am in a boat when I could be with her?

What is beauty? Some would say, she is old as the oldest stone. I say, *she earned every wrinkle, every slow sure step, and every ache.* She creaks as much as this wooden boat. I miss her and I miss how her hair would flap in wind loosely as these square sails.

Beauty is not absolute, and changes from man to man to woman to woman, different as ocean waves, different as a boat caught in the rise and settling of waves, different as amount in the sails or the absence of wind.

I remember the early days, the pitch of our marriage bed and the calmness after.

        A boat in ocean
        is never in the beginning
        or middle or end

Sneewittchen

Jane Yolen

She looks in the mirror wondering
Where is the magic?
Sees the age lines,
little sandpiper tracks
across her cheeks,
under the sunken eyes.
The tales promised more,
but there is no more,
only broken veins which
make a map of her face.

Surely someone wants to search
her surfaces, wants to plunge
into her cold rivers, wants
to set a finger wandering
along the blue roads on her breasts?

Mirror, mirror, she whispers,
but the magic, like her youth,
is long gone and even as she looks,
her face cracks like the mirror
into a thousand shards of glass.

Showcase

Timothy Green
Dipika Mukherjee
Don Share

Poetry, Fractalized:
Featuring Poet Timothy Green

by Elizabeth Nichols

Timothy Green is the editor behind the prolific and award-winning poetry magazine *Rattle*. While many know Green for his editing prowess, he is also a poet in his own right—a poet whose work has been described as "the gift of passion" with "fire at its core." Indeed, Green's work is rooted in a kind of emotional hotbed and he chooses words and images as if picking stars out of a nebula. For Green, just as with the magazine he works for, poetry must be without pretension. As such, his poetry is accessible. It is less stanza and meter than it is a musical, emotionally resonant experience. Even when Green centers his work around a geometric concept, a fractal, he grounds that concept in earthy, heady images like "light rain" that "speaks any language." It is not an exaggeration to say that Green is the Studs Terkel of poetry, telling the story of the every man with a deft, empathetic pen.

Green is a graduate of the University of Rochester and notably earned an award from the American Academy of Poets as a student. In 2004, Green's life took a shift from working in group home for adults with schizophrenia when he moved to Southern California to become an assistant editor of *Rattle*. Green would later become the editor for *Rattle* and in 2009 release his own collection, *American Fractal*.

American Fractal was Green's master's thesis at the University of Southern California, where he graduated with a degree in professional writing. Indeed, *American Fractal* showcases Green at the height of his talents. Of his first chapbook, Green said, "At some point it occurred to me that there was a fractal nature to the system—that the dynamics scale up congruently as you progress from the personal to the familial to the national to the global. Because the same patterns repeat, they can all be seen as metaphors for each other." Green's collection is a study in the repetition of form and image to create meaning within meaning, layering voices together to create an *American Fractal*. In this resonant collection, Green's poems crystalize into larger thematic metaphors. Readers are treated to a kaleidoscopic experience that defines an ever-shifting American identity. It is therefore perfectly fitting that as a preface to section four of the collection, Green quotes Robert Frost: "America is hard to see."

In the titular poem of Green's singular collection, the form of the poem reflects the theme of the fractal. Green's lines are grouped into fragments of words, pieces of images, that combine together to create the meaning of the poem. The structure recalls the geometric basis of the fractal itself. Apart from "American Fractal," other poems in collection repeat this same structure, including "The Body," "Her Face Once," "Cutlery," "Vigilance: What You'll Miss," and "The Bending of Birches." This repetition of form exemplifies Green's mastery of the manipulation of poetic form to imbue and reinforce the meaning of his images and words. "American Fractal," in particular, is an almost psychedelic tour of the mind in all its sharp vivacity, color, and noise. Each group of words is an image, a single thought or emotion, which build into a message. "American Fractal" is life in all its messy horror and beauty:

From "American Fractal"

two mirrors face each other   my hands over my face   the

porcelain soap dish   an angel's wing's & a mile of its offerings

pink on pink on black tile I'm in the bathroom   close the door

shut the light   down the hall tv too loud   bob barker & the

price is right   shut that out too   I'm on the edge of

something   of adulthood   of a gulf a canyon looking

down down   no vultures circling picking bones though   no

heaped bodies to climb over   no fall to cushion   or to be

cushioned   not the body that matures this time just this

hollow wooden door

...

...what don't we hold onto? mother in the living room on the couch *shake her shake her* *wake her up* & father at the

bar he says late at work he says & the bathroom with its cheap lock that convenient clasp & the light on & the light off & the mirror into mirror into mirror that silver-backed glass looking like her looking like him the images playing off themselves in the glass *divide divide* & how could they know each one each image into infinity how could they know? each image one moment behind the last catching up & catching up until the last & finally letting go the last like a leap into no faith letting go that smallest star that grain of sand that simplest & finest point of light

Green's work also uses real subjects as inspiration. His poem "Fifty-Hour Online Gaming Binge Proves Fatal" was written in memory of Lee Seong Seop, a young South Korean man who walked into an internet café and died while playing the popular video game Star Craft for almost fifty consecutive hours. Green takes this real-life tragedy of game addiction, and immortalizes Seop with evocative imagery: "…Some kinds / of men just live inside their heads, like bass / thrown back twice, like flies in love with fly sheets. / … Like Lee, we choke down every little sweet / we find our eyes on any stone that shines / as if this bit of light could never last." Similarly, "Man Auctions Ad Space on Forehead" is based on a BBC news article from 2005 that reports the story of Andrew Fischer, who wanted to sell the advertising space on his forehead to the highest bidder on eBay. Once again, Green transforms this real story into a piece of lyricism:

From "Man Auctions Ad Space on Forehead"

...

Everyone was talking; it was the new parlor game—
what would you make him wear for the rest of his life?

A middle finger? The Yin-Yang? Would you be
generous? Would you use a scarlet font? Or maybe

would you have them print this poem. Have them print it
in a slanted scrawl, like a secret encephalogram, too

tiny to read. Let him be free and rich and happy. Let him
have a daughter some day, look down for the first time

at the plainness of her soft skull, her pristine scalp,
most infinite of possibilities only the wealthy can afford.

Perhaps, however, Green's best work happens when he blends reality with surrealism. When he builds dreamlike landscapes, and lets readers enter a realm of poetic magical realism. Much of American Fractal, in fact, is a mix of stuff of life and the stuff that dreams are made of. Green's poem "After Hopper" is a perfect example of a real subject turned poetic fever dream. "After Hopper" is inspired by Edward Hopper's famous, and often parodied, 1942 realist painting Nighthawks. In "After Hopper," Green fleshes out the life of the iconic woman in the red dress sitting in the downtown diner in Nighthawks. He gives her a voice, and a depth of character that rouses the senses and the soul:

From "After Hopper"

She says that everything is after Hopper.
That posh hotel—you looked about to slap her,
but never did. Sometimes she'd wait at night
in her blue robe, face folded like the note
you didn't leave crumpled in a coat pocket.

...

She says you never see her talk,
but just about to talk, about to smile.
She says every moment is a jail;
this diner is her prison of endless light—
yet no one moves. Her cigarette remains
unlit. The busboy doesn't lift his hands.
You could write a thousand lines, she says,
on all the things she never does or has.
How she seems so sad she might have cried.
How you only ever see her almost satisfied.

The reader is enveloped the smoky atmosphere of a noir poem. The woman in the red dress addresses the reader directly, and the reader is suddenly inserted into and invested in the life of a woman birthed from talent and oil paint. Once again, Green has created an emotionally resonant experience with imagery and lyricism. He has created an accessible poem without pretension. And he has demonstrated his profound talent as a poet. In Green's poetry, life is an awesome mixture of reality and dreams—a fractalized metaphor upon metaphors where everything is related and illuminated.

In Conversation with Timothy Green

Interviewed by Elizabeth Nichols

Thank you for answering these questions, and sharing your insights with our Pirene's Fountain readers. It is a treat to speak with you both as editor of the acclaimed poetry magazine *Rattle* and as a poet yourself.

1. You've been an editor at *Rattle* for over a decade now. What kinds of things did you implement at *Rattle* early on and what kinds of things have you experimented with or added in the years since?

I try to add something new every year or so, both to keep the magazine feeling fresh and also to keep myself from getting bored. The first thing I did was start the *Rattle* Poetry Prize, which is hopefully one of the best single-poem poetry contests in the world, with a $10,000 award. Then I added newsletter issues in PDF form that ended up being 50 pages long. Then we started publishing poems online daily instead of by issue, then switched from biannual to quarterly print publication, then started publishing an annual young poets anthology, then the Poets Respond news poems, then the Ekphrastic Challenge, then the Wrightwood Literary Festival, then most recently the Rattle Chapbook Prize.

Not everything has worked, though. For the entire stretch, I've been trying to find a way to include reviews of poetry books in a way that people other than friends and family of the poets would actually read. I tried making them personal and casual, so hopefully more engaging. I tried moving them online to make them more timely and sharable. I tried making them very short microreviews, hoping that would work well with Twitter-age attention spans. Nothing has been successful, though, as far as web-traffic and reader-response. Everyone just likes reading poems, I've found. But I do have one more plan, which might end up being next year's new project, so stay tuned, I guess …

2. There is a stereotypical view of poetry as a something esoteric and gated. To some extent, this view still exists. And that's why *Rattle* is so refreshing as a magazine concerned with poetry that speaks to everyone, not just poetry lauded in scholarship or in award circles. In many ways, this central tenet of *Rattle* is reminiscent of Studs Terkel's great 1974 book *Working*, which collected oral histories from everyday working people from all walks of life, giving them a platform to share their story. As an editor, how do you ensure that "poetry without pretension" always takes precedence at *Rattle*?

> I'm not familiar with that book, I'll have to check it out! It's not very hard to avoid pretentious poetry, because we all find pretentious poetry to be pretty boring. We have four editors involved in selecting poems, and none of us had any desire to be poets or professors in any serious way. None of us care a wit about literary scholarship. We just enjoy hearing about people's lives and their insights on the world, in the condensed, musical, memorable space that a poem creates. Rattle's founder, Alan C. Fox, is a businessmen and lawyer. Asha Fox is a reporter and news anchor. Megan Green and I read everything that's submitted, but Alan and Asha only read what we bring to editorial meetings. We pitch what we want to publish, and they serve as our ideal readers, which helps to keep our tastes from getting too odd or esoteric. When you read 150,000 poems a year, things that are strange start to stand out a little more than maybe they should. We need some grounding from time to time.

3. In an interview with Connie Post, featured on the website "The Review Review," you state that, "In the age of information and the swamp of Facebook, with smartphones always in our hands…poetry becomes an increasingly valuable respite from the constant, shallow stimulation." Moreover, you affirm, "That thoughtful, quiet, reflective, meditative, empathetic place we go to when we read or write a poem is the cure to so many of society's ailments right now." Much has been said about the power of poetry along these lines, but what is it, in your opinion, about poetry specifically that makes it a panacea for modern life?

> Well, for starters, poetry is the antithesis of modern life. It's reflective rather than reflexive; it's deep and private and still. It's also astonishingly old. Whereas the earliest proto-writing developed 9,000 years ago as pictograms on tortoise shells in northern China, the oral language is

hundreds of thousands of years older. Recent research of bone structures suggests that Neanderthals had complex speech, which would mean modern human speech likely developed even farther up the Homo lineage. The oral tradition of storytelling might be 500,000 years old. And with no other way to record them, the most important stories were almost certainly fixed in poem and song—in the rhythms and repetitions of speech. So poetry is in our DNA—literally. Poetry is in our epigenetic ancestral memory of narrative archetypes, but it's even deeper than that—poetry has shaped the structure of our brains. It's how we've evolved to make sense of the world. If you consider something like the profound symbolism in the story of Adam and Eve—which passed from one storyteller to the next for probably 30,000 years before anyone had the ability to write it down—that's poetry, and we're drawn to it innately to this day.

And then, too, I think composing a poem is the ultimate act of meditation. We don't meditate even informally much, as a culture, and that's a real problem. The constant intrusion of technological stimulation leaves very little time for quieting the mind. I believe that anything we do in which we're fully engaged is meditative—anything that allows the self to dissolve into the oneness of the universe is a kind of mediation. That includes things like playing music or sports, or gardening, or cooking, which is why, when you're engaging with those activities that you enjoy, your concept of time changes; hours pass by unnoticed and you lose yourself. I think we need that mental calm in the same way we need physical sleep, and poetry is especially good at this. Poetry lives exactly on that creative line between order and chaos—that's why poetry is often revelatory. It's perhaps the most reliable way to construct a religious space in a secular world. To me, even as an atheist, poetry is spiritual. And as the religious tradition necessarily fades away in our enlightenment, we need those alternative headwaters of spirituality more and more. God is dead, but maybe poetry can fill in some of the gaps.

4. In regard to your own writing, your poems and short stories have appeared in numerous online and print publications, but *American Fractal* is your first full length collection. What was the impetus behind *American Fractal*? Did you have any themes or subjects in mind for the collection?

Having studied abnormal psychology in college, and working afterward at a group home for adults with schizophrenia, I found myself exploring the collective manifestations of psychological disorders in society through the poems I was writing. At some point it occurred to me that there was a fractal nature to the system—that the dynamics scale up congruently as you progress from the personal to the familial to the national to the global. Because the same patterns repeat, they can all be seen as metaphors for each other. So, as I was writing about my own personal experiences with mental illness, I found I could also simultaneously write about collective-scale neuroses—like, for example, the paranoia inherent within the military-industrial complex. All of that sounds extremely academic and pretentious, I'm sure, but those were the ideas I was mulling over as I was writing about people I knew and experiences I've had growing up—the book probably doesn't read at all as pretentious, I don't think, and on one level it's very accessible, but there's a layer exploring broader concepts, and it is what it is.

5. Tell us, if you could, a bit about your writing process. What inspires your poetry? What makes a poem effective for you?

Because the act of writing is so tied up for me with meditation and the pursuit of transcendent consciousness, let's say, I don't like to know what I'm writing about or where the poem is going. I think a lot of poets would say that it starts with an itch, some kind of phrase or idea that resonates but doesn't quite resolve, and then you write the poem as a way to try to find it's resolution. Maybe it's an emotion that you can't quite source, or an idea that you can't quite articulate. I think that's how it tends to work. I think if you stare at the blank page long enough and let yourself daydream, creativity tends to start happening on its own.

6. On your personal website, timothy-green.org, the quote "No aim is necessary; nothing is true" is featured in your banner. What significance does this quote have for you, and does it inform your writing in some way?

Yes, that's exactly what I was trying to get at with the last question. That's a line from a poem I wrote—I can't remember whether or not it's published anywhere—but I use that as a touchstone to remind myself, in confronting the page, that none of it really matters. It's a reference to some lines in *Zen in the Art of Archery*: "The right art is purposeless, aimless! The more obstinately you try to learn how to shoot the arrow for the sake of hitting the goal, the less you will succeed in the one, and the further the other will recede. What stands in your way is that you have a much too willful will. You think that what you do not do yourself does not happen." I think that's the best creative writing advice. I also like how Bukowski put it on his tombstone, though: "Don't try."

7. In an interview with Jendi Reiter of the website "Winning Writers," you describe the best poetry as resonant: "it lodges itself somewhere in your gut, or maybe your soul, and rumbles and grumbles and buzzes in there for the rest of your life." What poems continue to rumble, grumble, and buzz in your life?

Oh there are so many poems, it's hard to narrow them down into a list. My recall is terrible, so if you asked me to recite as many poems as I could, I might be able to come up with a half-dozen on the spot. But throughout the day, most days, any time I'm daydreaming, waiting in line, driving in the car, something will trigger a poem to emerge out of the depths and I'll run through it in my head like remembering a song from childhood. The most frequent on the play list are probably E.E. Cummings' "Into the Strenuous Briefness," Stevens' "The Snow Man," Brigit Pegeen Kelly's "Song," Charles Wright's translation of Montale's "Freeing a Dove," Richard Wright's haiku "Just enough of rain," Li-Young Lee's "Seven Happy Endings," Kim Addonizio's "The Sound." But that's only what's coming to me at the moment. The two most recent additions are Zeina Hashem Beck's pair from Poets Respond: "Ya'aburnee" and "Ghazal: Back Home." Unlike the others, it's Zeina's voice playing in my head instead of my own, because I've listened to the recordings enough times.

I just realized that the first poem I mentioned was by E.E. Cummings. If you asked Alan the same question, he would definitely say "anyone who lived in a pretty how town." That probably tells you something about Rattle's tastes right there—we think Cummings is vastly underrated when he wasn't being gimmicky.

8. With *American Fractal* under your belt, do you have any plans for future collections or projects?

 To be honest, I haven't made any plans or had any ambitions since American Fractal. After that collection was published, I started working on a few different book projects, but writing for publication and the thought of being an author started to really bum me out. When I began writing, before ending up at *Rattle,* it was just for fun—it was a meditative mental exercise, and that's all it was, and I loved it. Thinking about readings and reviews and manuscripts and author photos quickly sucked the joy out. Writing poems knowing in the back of my mind that someone was going to read them made me not want to write poems. So I stopped for a while. Then I started again, but I don't send them anywhere. I've made exactly two submissions since 2008, both on the same day, on a whim—I sent a short story to *The New Yorker* and a set of poems to *Poetry*. All rejected, of course. At this point, I usually don't even send poems when people ask for them—I mean to, and then never follow through. I have a folder full of them, and I assume at some point I'll get the urge to do something with them all, but for now I don't even care to look. I'd much rather be publishing and promoting the work of other poets, and the act of poetry itself. And my top priority above that is being a husband, and father to a three- and a seven-year-old—so maybe it's a stage of life thing.

Thank you for your time and insightful responses, Timothy! It was a pleasure to interview you.

 Thank you, the pleasure was all mine.

Featuring
Dipika Mukherjee

by Lark Vernon Timmons

"There's something beautifully kinetic about a pen gliding over white space."

Respected author, poet and sociolinguist Dipika Mukherjee first saw her byline in black-and-white on the children's page of her Wellington, New Zealand newspaper at the age of ten or eleven; a clipping of the early accolade still hangs in her parents' home in New Delhi, India. At a time when she felt ugly, awkward and experienced racist bullying, she admits seeing her name in print was addictive: "Writing was my refuge and gave me a standing among my peers."

Well-read, Well-traveled, Well-versed

"My days are divided into chunks of activity punctuated by a lot of dreaming and reading."

As the daughter of an Indian diplomat posted to Geneva, Switzerland, her father's career would take Mukherjee beyond her native India to New Zealand, Indonesia, and Malaysia.

Among her wealth of writing are two poetry collections, *The Third Glass of Wine* (Writer's Workshop, 2015) and chapbook *The Palimpsest of Exile* (Rubicon Press, 2009); short story collections; *The Rules of Desire* (Fixi, Malaysia, 2015); and three edited anthologies of Southeast Asian short stories, *Champion Fellas* (2016), *Silverfish New Writing* (2006) and *The Merlion and Hibiscus* (2012).

Poets With Fierce Voices

> Write your words! Then, loudly breathe them out,
> harness your voice, let them journey on,
> sound them like dandelion bells, like all
> nuisance weeds, somersaulting breeze, flowering
> minds, restless in the wind; life's puffed-up
> wholeness and underside merrily
> changeable. Don't clutch them, palm-jailed,
> offerings only for the worthy,
> until all mangled and diminished
> crushed in closed pages they pine
> like false promises of unrequited love.
>
> sangamhouse.org 2015

"Poetry comes more naturally to me than any other form of writing."

Mukherjee's scholarly work focuses on the intersections between language policy and migrant groups in Malaysia. Dipika, who is multi-lingual, has taught language and linguistic courses in China, India, the Netherlands, United States, Malaysia and Singapore. She holds a doctorate in English from Texas A&M University.

Most recently, her debut novel, *Thunder Demons,* longlisted for the Man Asian Literary Prize (Gyanna, 2011), was republished as *Ode to Broken Things* (Repeater, 2016). Her second novel, *Shambala Junction* (Aurora Metro, 2016), won the Virginia Prize for Fiction.

Regarding her ability to cross literary genres with ease, she responds with a lighthearted and fitting reference to Bengali path-lighter and poet, Tagore, who "wrote in every conceivable genre and started painting in his seventies."

Mukherjee says writing poetry, short stories and novels all involve different processes, but each of the creative genres she works in feed off each other. Poetry resuscitates her soul when she's exhausted by a novel. Sometimes tiring of the brevity of short fiction, she needs to spend some time on a longer work, even if it is an academic paper. One constant is the her practice of writing regularly "so the Muse knows exactly where she is when she decides to visit."

> I find my muse as much
> as she finds me, without
> home or temple, veena
> in hand, book in another,
> in the feminine infinite we
> make our home.
>
> Excerpt from "Migration, Exile...These are Men's Words"
> First published in Sugarmule, May 2013

Novel Approach

Dr. Mukherjee recalls that writing her first novel, Thunder Demons, was a bit like donning the mantle of Sisyphus, and the journey to publication was no different. As a permanent resident of Malaysia with a son and husband who held Malaysian citizenship, she wanted to address her country's iniquities—specifically, events involving power brokers.

"I'm not interested in writing...exotic stories about beautiful immigrants with bare-shouldered women in glamourous saris on the cover."

The pungent, noisy world of baby-trafficking

Shambala Junction was initially inspired by an article Mukherjee read in an Indian community newsletter in Houston which described babies for sale in India, where international adoptions were benefiting from the misery of Indian families. Recognizing her ability as a South Asian woman to be a voice for the many still silenced, she wrote the first draft in several months.

"I try to write about socially relevant issues and open up a dialogue about taboo topics."

Turn Away

>...two teenage girls were gang-raped and then hanged from a tree in a village in the northern state of Uttar Pradesh...

>Reuters, Thu May 29, 2014

>from hemp ropes on slender necks, the embroidery glinting on a kameez, let susurrations visit the unrooted. Was the younger almost asleep, tunelessly humming, when the older hissed, Come, I need to go now, water-can in hand towards malignant fields? The villagers squat on dusty haunches, think of moonglint on unfastened buckles, khaki pants, the thrust of earth rising. There is anger, and lewd spectacle, in the gaze of old men.

>Sing, sing the myths of Mother Earth unzippered as refuge. Oh, Mithya – Lies! — look, babies unshoveled into the earth only blossom into meat, swinging from the sky.

>   (First published in The Aerogram, August 2014)

Certainly we see Mukherjee's fearlessness as a writer in her prose poem, "Turn Away." Also evident is her ability to pen passionate visuals:

Guan Yin In The Huangshan

>The Yellow Mountains tower and swoop like eagles,
>with ragged rocks like stalagmite claws,
>and feathery pine trees.
>In the North Sea area a tall rock pierces the sky
>like a caped woman with a lotus in her hand;
>It's the Guan Yin Peak.
>
>The pilgrims all stop here.
>
>Lovers lock locks then throw away keys,
>red ribbons of wishes flutter in the breeze.
>But it is only a rock to my eye, maybe shaped like a woman
>not so unlike others springing from the mountains,
>so many could be slim goddesses;
>Then the guide says, closing his eyes,
>One can see her only Here...he strikes a fist on his heart.
>In the Huangshan Mountains, a photo is taken
>of a blood-red sky torn birthing the sun,
>from Brightness Top, the peaks are shadowed black,
>but one, the Guan Yin peak, stands haloed round the head
>centering the light, unmistakably woman-figured,
>lotus in her hand.
>
>Sometimes the third eye is a camera,
>sometimes a fist to the heart.
>
> Sugarmule Volume #43

I am enamored by Dipika's lyrical verse for a dozen reasons, especially for its sensory elements and lilt:

Mountain Echoes

In Bhutan, the mountains call with peals
of prayer bells, mantras churned by brooks
as pilgrims trek a weary path
to the Taktsang Dzong, where a holy man
soared to heavenly heights
on the back of his woman tiger.
Legends spring from rocks here,
of the eternal through ambrosial waters The Buddha looms large in
bhumisparshamudra,
touching earth, rooted here.

Yellow tsatsas, in the red shade of spinning wheels,
mingle cremated ashes into dusty clay,
flags flutter a rainbow salvation,
as two little girls, like kittens in the sun
settle next to me, on the wide rock,
the older speaks haltingly, the younger not at all
yet we play scissors-paper-stone
they teach me Dzongkha, gymtse-dho-shoko
grabbing hands to cut, cover and swallow whole;
it's a language of flashing fingers,
palms turning black-and-white, nap-ya-karp
human babble jostling in amity.

I want them to win.
To always reach out
with such grace, such openness,
to gesture of crows-spider-horses,
to encapsulate a living world
in such mellifluous hands
within tiny folded palms.

Their laughter peals like the prayer bell
over these sheer cliffs, kissed by moist clouds
drenched in holy waters.

poemhunter.com 2016

"Poetry is the one thing that has never abandoned me."

These Days

Like all writers, Dipika speaks of the need for a certain amount of uninterrupted "mindspace," and shares she has always cherished writing at night. These days, without the demands of young children and family concerns, she says she can literally write for days—and loves these blissful stretches in her own home so much she calls them "mini residencies."

"Feed your soul every single day by being grateful for this life that you once yearned for, and is now becoming a reality because you never gave up."

Sincere thanks to PF's 2016 Liakoura Award winner, Dr. Mukherjee for her time, talent and kind permissions.

In Conversation With
Dipika Mukherjee

Interviewed by Lark Vernon Timmons

Dipika, it's a privilege being able to connect with you and share your vast and varied contribution to the field of writing with our readers!

Thank you for inviting me to address Pirene's readers!

What was your most significant "take-away" as a first-time novelist with the publication of *Thunder Demons?* How has your experience of the re-publication of the novel—now *Ode to Broken Things*—compare to the first time around?

Thunder Demons had been longlisted for the Man Asian Literary Prize, so I chose to go with a very young publisher (Gyaana, Divya Dubey) who was just starting out in Indian publishing. I envisioned us growing together, rather like Amitav Ghosh had successfully done with his Delhi publisher. Divya is an amazing & motivated entrepreneur (she received a British Council citation for excellence in publishing) but the company was too new to deal with the vast and complicated market of Indian publishing. There were HUGE distribution issues. I am glad I had sold only South Asian rights to Gyaana, but even within that small market of six countries, *Thunder Demons* was not available in major bookshops unless I had launched the book there.

Ode to Broken Things was published by Repeater Press in London and they specialize in the publication of edgy political books, so my work was handled with much care by my editor, Tariq Goddard. Repeater Books uses Penguin/Random House to distribute books in the US and Simon & Schuster in Australia, so they have an amazing distribution system worldwide. The book sold out in the UK within three months and was reprinted; now it is available in print, in large print, as an audiobook, and also in braille. I love that I can walk up to the local Barnes and Nobles in Chicago and see my book on the shelves – having a good distribution network for your work is SO important, but I had to learn that over years of experience. Check on who is distributing your books; that was my takeaway from publishing my first novel.

I am fascinated by author Toni Morrison's assertion that "all good art is political," and wonder if you could share what these words mean for you as they relate to the characters you develop and socio-political issues you bring to the page?

I feel, as an Asian woman with a voice, that my writing has to be political; it has to go beyond artful words. I see so many problems around me (racism, gender inequality, female foeticide, disparity in border policing issues, migration, exile, among others) and although I cannot solve the world's problems, I see no point in writing pretty prose without a message. Choosing to ignore the issues of the day is also a political decision, but I see why writers self-censor under different regimes. I write about Malaysia and India and China and the Netherlands and the US...every place I have lived and worked in feeds my fiction and poetry. Although I belong to two of the most populous democracies (the US and India), I have to be aware of the perils of "free" speech, especially in the current political climate. What is hardest for me as a writer is to get off a soapbox; good art cannot lecture but must strive to entertain or astonish in some way, but that is hard to do when there is a rage simmering in your breast.

Because you are so adept at writing in various genres, have you ever considered screenwriting? Any possibility that *Ode to Broken Things,* or your second novel *Shambala Junction,* could make that leap from book to the big screen?

I would love to see these books on the screen, but no, I have not considered screenwriting! I think screenwriting requires a very specialized eye, a more visual (plus dramatic) writing style, and I'm not confident of my skills in that area.

Your education, travels and writing credentials are far-reaching and impressive. Tell us about the field in which you earned your Ph.D., and how it fits into the scheme of all things literary and academic.

I have a doctorate in Sociolinguistics from Texas A&M University and my academic work has investigated language change in Malaysia, the Netherlands and China. I love the rule-based fieldwork of linguistics, which is so different from creative writing. I think that is how I keep sane –by switching from one to the other –so that there is no monotony, only constant astonishment. Whether you are looking at how human beings use language to structure societies and communities, or interweave ancient fables and mythology into a novel, you learn so much about the boundlessness of the human imagination.

Regarding the languages you speak fluently—Bengali, Bangla, English, Hindi and Urdu—which came first? Could you educate us on the difference between dialect and language? Also, have you had occasion to work in any capacity as a foreign language translator?

Bengali is my mother tongue, so it is my first language. My father, a diplomat, was posted to Geneva when I was six months old, so French was also an early language although it has almost disappeared with disuse! We linguists like to define language as a dialect with an army an a navy; the only thing that differentiates the two is the political might of a nation which forms a language, often a national language, as opposed to a dialect. Mandarin Chinese and the other Chinese dialects (Cantonese, Hokkien etc) are not mutually intelligible, yet they are considered dialects whereas Hindi and Urdu are essentially the same but one is the national language of India and the other one of Pakistan. A lot of political weight comes to bear in the designations of language versus dialect.

I have not formally worked as a foreign language translator in print, but I work in Chicago with a group that helps migrants needing language services to apply for government benefits.

After encountering the charming photo on the Internet of you alongside His Holiness the Dalai Lama, there is no way I can resist asking about both the journey and the photograph!

It took me about four years of trying to meet His Holiness the Dalai Lama before it actually happened! I even wrote an essay about my unsuccessful attempt (https://chicagoliterati.com/2014/08/19/a-journey-to-the-dalai-lama-by-dipika-mukherjee/)

My third novel begins in the voice of a Buddhist monk about to immolate himself, so I travelled to McLeodgunj twice, to get a sense of the lives of Tibetans in exile. McLeodgunj is a gorgeous town nestled among the mountains and is also the home of the Dalai Lama, who is currently in exile in India. I met the Dalai Lama in 2015 and it was truly amazing and humbling experience, beyond anything I had imagined. He has a wonderful gentle humor which puts a visitor at ease immediately, and he teasingly challenged me to a linguistic duel to decide whether my Mandarin was worse than his Hindi. I was so tongue tied I could barely speak in English so I declined to lay out my awful Chinese language skills. He was an absolute delight and that meeting will always have a very special place in my heart.

Thanks so much for your time! I'll wrap with a pleasure-reading inquiry: what's atop your desk and/or bedside table waiting to be read?

Right now I am reading Tana French's *The Likeness;* Amitav Ghosh's *The Great Derangement; Em and the Big Hoom* by Jerry Pinto; Buku Fixi's *Little Basket 2017: New Malaysian Writing; Selected Poems* by Thomas Lux.

Featuring
Poetry Editor Don Share

by Linda Kim

Editor. Poet. Translator. A quintessential craftsman. Don Share is the chief editor of *Poetry*, the nation's oldest poetry magazine. Not only is his own work acclaimed, but he is one of the most renowned literary magazine editors in recent memory. Share is passionate about the curation of American poetry. While having a keen eye on up-and-coming modern poetry, he maintains a respectful awareness of past traditions. He keeps a finger on the pulse of national consciousness. Having spent so much of his life in pursuit of editorial work for various publications, Share has spent most of his life in service to others, to readers, and to the poetic field at large.

It's why he knows poetry isn't dead. "Poetry is alive and singing, and kicking and screaming, too," he says. In fact, he can't recall a "more vital time for poetry." It will survive.

In his long career, Share has gained extensive editorial experience. He has been with *Poetry* magazine since 2007 as a Senior Editor until he became its chief editor in 2013. Previously, he had been the Curator of the Poetry Room at Harvard University and Poetry Editor for *Harvard Review*. He was once a contributing editor for *Salamander*, Poetry Editor for *Partisan Review*, and Editor-in-Chief of *Literary Imagination: the Review of the Association of Literary Scholars and Critics*. He taught or lectured at various institutions, such as Harvard University, Lesley University, Boston University, and Oxford University. He was also on the advisory board of *Tuesday; An Art Project*.

With the breadth of his experience and involvement in the literary community, it's no wonder Share received no less than three National Magazine Awards for editorial excellence. He has gained other awards, too, in recognition of his contributions to American literature.

His own books of poetry include *Union, Squandermania,* and *Wishbone.* He is the editor of *Bunting's Persia* and a critical edition of Basil Bunting's poetry, as well as the co-editor of *The Open Door: 100 Poems, 100 Years of Poetry Magazine.* As a centennial celebration of Poetry, that latter book summarizes the sheer impact of the magazine by perfectly encapsulating a timeline of American poetry. Additionally, Share is an esteemed translator. His translations include *Seneca in English, Field Guide: Poems by Dario Jaramillo Agudelo,* and two collections of Miguel Hernández's poetry, the second of which won both the Times Literary Supplement Translation Prize and the Premio Valle Inclán for Spanish Translation.

His skill at translating foreign verse is evident in how he retains the spirit of Hernández's poetry:

"You Threw Me a Bitter Lemon" by Miguel Hernández

You threw me a bitter lemon
from a hand so warm and pure
that I tasted the bitterness
without spoiling it architecture.

With a yellow jolt, my sweet
and lazy blood turned hot, possessed,
and so I felt the bite
of the tip of that long, firm teat.

But glancing at you and seeing the smile
that this lemon condition produced
(so at odds with my greed and guile),

my blood blacked out inside my shirt,
and through that porous golden breast
I felt a pointed, dazzling hurt.

This translation shows how much Share is attracted to poignant verse. The rest of his translations prove just as powerful as they do here, rife as they are with stunning implications. His passion for Spanish verse comes alive through the way he makes the poem deeply personal, as if it were his own. He greatly admires Hernández, whose worldview is grounded in a way that Share takes inspiration from and applies to his own poetry. It was by reading poets like Hernández early in his youth that he learned the beauty of astonishing poetic turns and the pleasure of surprise—a fascination that would follow him throughout his life.

Writing is an impulse. Share also often thinks of and admires Irish poet Patrick Kavanagh when the latter says, "there was some kink in me, put there by Verse." This assertion resonates with Share. The words of Yeats and Auden similarly stick with him. He understands the quintessential truth that we turn to verse in tragic times because it is uniquely capable of revealing words about the unnameable. There is agency is being able to name otherwise unspoken and unknowable feelings. His own melancholic yet humorous poetry reflects the tragicomedy of life, as well as the beauty and solace found in ordinary things. There is relief in that and catharsis.

Having grown up in Memphis, Tennessee, with all its rich culture and musicality, Share is deeply aware of prosody and sound. His poems are layered in musical textures that play with words for the sake of experimentation. His books aren't afraid to mix and match epigrams and puns, sonnets and couplets, lamentations with other long free-verse forms. His profound phrasings are unique, humorous, and intimately sympathetic. At times funny, at other times poignant and tragic, the rhythms and narrative developments of his poetry never fail to astonish. Tension is sustained through the whiplash tones of comic relief and cutting humor, a tonal trademark beget from that delicate balancing act.

His first poetry collection, *Union,* was a finalist for the Boston Globe/PEN-New England Winship Award for outstanding book. Its title succinctly sums up its thematic tensions between the personal and the political, the domestic space with the public one, by focusing on unions and their dissolutions. Childhood transitions into adulthood, a first marriage is formed and broken, and identity is molded and reshaped to the backdrop of regional estrangement; the American South and the North stand in stark opposition each other. "Where the United States ends / and begins / The Mississippi is / a long American wound."

Share's first poetry book establishes the foundations of his life by setting up a contrast between his hometown of Memphis with New York to which he arrives in as an out-of-place stranger like so much adrift flotsam. Everything from his thick accent to his cold weather disinclinations alienates him, marks him as an outsider. The South's influence on his worldview is indelible, so the absence of any familiarity haunts his poems even when they're set in New York. In moving away from Tennessee and away from home for the first time, Share experiences a culture shock that deeply affects the perspectives of all his poetic speakers in all three of his books. The poet moves to where opportunities are, but Tennessee will forever remain with him.

After living in the Northeast, his begrudging relationship with the harsh "land of granite / and cod's head" continues, as his speakers grapple with regional divides. *Squandermania,* his second book, features poems worthy of praise in their depiction of regionalism. In fact, three poems had been nominated for a Pushcart Prize. Yet the poet's initial culture shock and discombobulation ends up manifesting here as a wry set of observations like when he concludes, "we can't help where we live / A Nor'easter."

From it syntax and diction to its usage of idioms, Share's poetry is undeniably American in style. The ways in which phrasings and images are pieced together remain consistently delightful. They are grounded in earnest speech and humorous tones, which otherwise uplift the melancholic regret of the book. The rhythms of life and climate in the North are pitted against the familiar South. Family, marriage, children, and Jewish ancestry are traced and rendered vividly as psychological landscapes. Interpersonal and generational conflicts reverberate as strongly as political ones. The conventions of language are as easily dismantled and deconstructed as the corrupt institutions of government.

Life is chaotic rather than orderly, predictable, and containable because it is messy, but there's solace to be found in its quiet moments as well. This philosophy is beautifully mirrored in the deconstruction of language, as well as the other myriad ways craft itself can reflect reality. He employs allusions, repetitions, tautologies, and a sense of relatable universality to keep readers engaged. Craft-wise, he is wise and it shows. Share can deftly manipulate both formal forms and free verse lines.

"The Mystery Letter"

What is the mystery letter
in the word, cry?
Why is monosyllable
not one?
At what age does one fail
to thrive?
When does the paring knife
lose its edge?
—How can you tell?
The last passenger pigeon flew
where, and left its brother doves...why?
What is the spirit of the letter,
the letter of the law?
The mystery letter is...why
the mystery?

Share interrogates the oddities and mysteries of language ceaselessly here, as he does in all of his poetry. The way he morphs and uses language makes it wholly personal and privatized in meaning but ambitious in scope. His wordplay is as flexible as his acute wit, his sharp observations, and his moving revelations.

His third poetry book, *Wishbone,* breaks away from the heaviness of *Squandermania* by unleashing the full extent of its experimentations and artful play. *Wishbone,* in particular, revels in the workings of craft, its possibilities, and its myriad deconstructions. An idiom is as likely to be raised up only to be quickly torn down in a multitude of ways.

More than ever the minutia of America speech is examined, parsed out, dissected, and then pieced together again. Share gives great weight to the worth of examining colloquial language. The influence of William Carlos Williams is undeniable here. Share as both a writer and an editor has always been keenly aware of past traditions in American poetry.

With a light touch, the book deploys an imaginative and whimsical approach in its portrayal of content and meaningful associations. Objects are displayed, examined, then juxtaposed into new collages. There's a playful irony in the compositions of opposition pieced together through prevalent couplets, and lineation tells a story where the absence of words say as much as the lines themselves.

"Rice in the Spoon"

Each in his house,
thinking of the key,

the locks, the windows,
doors, and roof.

In my sleep I lift
a finger. I see…

opposing blocks,
like Legos, in painful

composure of modes,
not moods.

Fake red feathers
fluffed in a spotted vase.

Sea glass beached
on a porch bench.

A brown bust
of a sad man.

A huge tin pitcher,
parched for years.

Rice glued to
a badly washed spoon.

Even the dust
quit moving to settle.

Even the snow is
a qualm, a sea.

There's an elevation in beauty in the most ordinary of things here that is reminiscent of Imagist sensibilities. This is an argument for a mode of looking, a type of contemplative gaze. The stunning effect of the collage here is to create new meaning, a brand new something out of nothing. It is an advocation for what can poetry achieve.

Years ago, the poet jumped at the chance to work at *Poetry* magazine. Though it required him to leave his position at Harvard and move to Chicago, he did so without hesitation. The reinvigoration of that career move shows in the poetic work of *Wishbone*. It stands out from his previous books in how it glorifies the locality of Chicago, reveling in its variety of characters, landscapes, and textures. Its verse practically shouts with confidence and glee, as it bursts with creativity. As a poet, he has always been inspired by his surroundings.

"If a poem isn't a surprise, then it isn't a poem," he says. Share's own work holds up to this philosophy well, as he plays with all the oddities of language. He seeks in his own writing what he seeks in the work of others.

As a reader and an editor, Share is self-taught. He never received a formal poetry education; instead, he learned by reading as much as he possibly could wherever he could. By working in a library in his foundational years, he was able to read the poetry shelves from A to Z. Or, as Share puts it, from "Auden to Zukofsky!" His love affair with libraries began then. Being self-taught gives Share an openminded perspective that freely accepts unorthodox conventions. In a way, his own poetry reflects this through its vers libre quality. He is voracious as a reader, refreshingly down to earth, and has a good sense of humor that seeps into all his poetry and work as an editor.

It makes *Poetry* the perfect place for him.

No matter the style or genre, *Poetry* has always aimed to print the best of American verse by new and established poets since its inception in 1912. Today, its issues are particularly acclaimed as a flawless blend of literature, verse, criticism, and visual arts like photography due in part to Don Share's editorial vision. Historically, the magazine hasn't restricted itself to any specific poetic movement or aesthetic. Its traditional "Open Door" policy is one that Share has always agreed with vigorously because in the past it had allowed poets like T.S. Eliot, Yeats, Marianne Moore, and Ezra Pound to flourish.

As an editor, Share is especially welcoming of openness and newness. He is always on the lookout for oddness in life to be reflected in the oddities of craft and language because "every time a poem connects with someone there's transcendence, there's innovation. There's no end to what can be imagined." As a child, poetry struck him as very mature "adult stuff, very grown-up," but now it is quite the opposite for him. In poetry, he has recovered a childlike delight in new things.

Share delights in new things. He searches for new and exciting poetry. He is open to strangeness, discomfort, and disconcertingly experimental poems so long as they push the boundaries of poetry forward. "As an editor I've never looked for any particular kind of work," he says, "only whatever surprised me. I don't publish things just because I like them, but rather when I learn something from them, or imagine that other people with different tastes from mine will."

While there's nothing in particular he looks for when reading submissions for *Poetry*, he constantly yearns to read something that defeats expectation. By purposefully not following a specific criteria, he prevents inherent biases from interfering with emergent new trends. Instead, he approaches each poem on its individual merit, examines what it uniquely and terrifically accomplishes on its own terms, and sees whether he can be affected in ways he could have never imagined.

On average, more than 150,000 poems are submitted to the magazine every year from around the world. Share devotes a quarter or a third of each issue to new poets. All of the issues he's edited have also included significant selections of translated foreign verse, exposing them to the English-speaking world. Consequently, Share has brought more diversity to the magazine by giving voice to emerging new talent no matter their origin. His belief that the magazine ought "to reflect what's really going on in poetry and in the world around us" manifests in the vibrancy of each issue.

At *Poetry* the content speaks for itself. A reputation built up in the span of a century brings with it the expectation that each issue should be superb. Share delivers each time, seemingly effortlessly, yet producing a magazine is difficult. There are meticulous steps to take during production. It's very hands-on work that adheres to a tight production schedule. It takes time to piece together the work of others into multiple magazine issues, with the process very much similar to publishing a book, and about four of them are worked on at a time.

After receiving submissions, Share and his fellow editors read and talk about them day after day. During the evaluation process, those accumulated prose and poem pieces rest on his desk as he ponders over their collective meaning, contemplating the intuitive ways they can be juxtaposed together in order to "create a sequence of works that are somehow in dialogue with each other."

Once the order and flow of an issue has been established, the design process can begin. A layout is finalized and a cover is made. Meanwhile all of the typesetting, copyediting, and proofreading must be done on time while digital and Braille versions of each issue are made. The magazine is then sent off to be properly printed, packaged, and delivered to subscribers and bookstores around the world. Even minute details about the paper stock used are carefully considered, such as its color, texture, and smell. This is especially important when the pages are focused on being visually appealing through beautiful covers, artwork, and a selection of poetry that is boldly performative or typographically experimental.

It's hard work, but completely rewarding.

As T. S. Eliot noted 50 years ago, "*Poetry*, in fact, is not a little magazine, but an institution." It not only discovers new voices, but it encourages them as well. Share works tirelessly to do the same. As the magazine's twelfth editor, he continues the long tradition of great editors being in touch with great American poets. He believes fervently in the magazine's mission, and thus provides support to others whenever he can because he believes that new opportunities should be created for those who haven't had them before. It's why he takes his work so seriously.

"The poem is a catalyst where you're bringing two different kinds of people together. And at its best, when it works, there's a kind of spark, and everyone comes away illuminated by what the spark has ignited."

And if Share coincidentally broadens the scope of the magazine in the process, then so much the better, but he remains humble. He is always quick to attribute his success at *Poetry* to his predecessors and to the hard work of his fellow staff members. In his eyes, his success is due less to his own credit than to the high quality blueprint he is merely following.

For him working with poetry is a privilege, and every issue brings with it its own joys. Reading poetry epitomizes the journey of discovery. And that sense of discovery is dearly important to Share. He wants to avert joyless poetry. He wants to be surprised and delighted anew with previously unknown possibilities in verse, and so guides *Poetry's* audiences to expect the unexpected. It's a philosophy that allows American poetry as a whole to grow. It's a philosophy that he himself follows in his own work.

At the end of the day, he wants to be surprised by what crosses his desk. "People really want to write poetry and be published, and this desire is something sacred."

In Conversation with Don Share

Interviewed by Ami Kaye

Rather than start with your writing journey, can you tell us how poetry found you?

Poetry tried, and *failed*, to find me when teachers of mine at an early age presented the old chestnuts in a joyless and rote way, and without regard to what might actually be intelligible - and joyful - to a young person. I have great sympathy for those tasked with teaching poetry to children; but it can be done wisely, without fuss or torment to child or teacher, and with verve. I don't actually think poetry goes looking for anybody, though. It's there when you're ready for it. I stumbled upon Robert Service's "The Cremation of Sam McGee" as a teenager, which I loved, being a kid in Tennessee - and I started writing ballads after reading a collection of his poems; then I heard the great American humorist Jean Shepherd read Don Marquis's fabled "archy and mehitabel" poems on the radio... and off I went to find all the rest of poetry. When I was 16, I got to see Allen Ginsberg in Memphis with a friend. He was the first living poet I ever laid eyes on - I suppose I thought they were all dead white guys with long grey beards. Ginsberg chanted OM for a long while, then played Blake songs on a harmonium before his reading - so it was two-for-one Ginsberg and Blake for me then, all ravishing. Then I began buying up the classic City Lights Pocket Poets books starting with *Howl* and *Kaddish*. I even hand printed a chapbook of my own stuff that I designed to be orange and blue, just like *Lunch Poems*. I also bought and cherished Edward Field's *Stand Up Friend With Me*, Delmore Schwartz's *Summer Knowledge* and books by Paul Blackburn and Auden and Melvin Tolson and May Sarton. After May Sarton, well, May Swenson. Had a crush on Sappho and Léonie Adams, Anne Sexton, and even, Lord forgive me, Sor Juana. Lorca, Gwendolyn Brooks, Nelly Sachs, Ashbery, Hugo, Bishop, Moore, Lowell, Wright, on and on, and I gobbled them up. I even got shit jobs in libraries just to read through entire poetry sections. It was a true education, and best of all no papers, and no grades! But I didn't see a living poet again till I was about twenty-five: Louise Glück. I was too shy to talk to her.

Chicago's thriving literary scene is certainly enriched by your presence. Tell us why you think Chicago is a good place for poetry and for you. Where else have you lived and worked before coming to Chicago?

Why, thank you. Chicago enriches me every single day. H.L. Mencken famously said: "I give you Chicago. It is not London and Harvard. It is not Paris and buttermilk. It is American in every chitling and sparerib. It is alive from snout to tail." He wasn't kidding, and though it can be a hard place, I love it here. I've lived in Tennessee (what Mencken called the Sahara of the Bozart!), Texas, Denmark, Rhode Island, and the Boston area, but this is the best for me. And it's the best for poetry, too. In other places I've lived and worked, you always had to worry about what some important local poetry figure thought; not here! You can think your own thoughts. There's no received wisdom here on any subject except sports and hotdogs, which is fair enough. *Poetry* magazine wouldn't have lasted 105 years if it had been located in New York or London or Paris or Boston. This is the place.

Why Basil Bunting? What was your fascination with him and his work?

An accident, to be honest, though a life-changing one. Back in about 2000, Geoffrey Hill and Christopher Ricks - two of my mentors and heroes! - started a graduate program to teach people how to do such things as textual editing, and so on. I was working in a great job - I was Curator of Poetry at Harvard University, and also Poetry Editor of both *Harvard Review* and the now-defunct *Partisan Review* - and they'd asked me to be the first doctoral student in the program. At first, I said no - "I've lived all my life without a Ph.D., and I don't need one now!" But then I realized it was a chance to work with Geoffrey and Christopher and the likes of the late William Arrowsmith and the legendary bibliographer Hugh Amory.... so I changed my mind! Once that was settled, the question arose of what my research topic would be. I floated a few ideas, one being a critical edition of the works of Lester Bangs (which I still think is a great idea); but Ricks demurred, perhaps sensibly. I had other ideas (an edition of George Gascoigne, which was a terrible idea as I'd have been way out of my depth - and a real scholar was already doing one!), none of which pleased him. In exasperation, Christopher asked me what I was reading right then and there; and I was reading Basil Bunting. I loved, and was fascinated by, Bunting - but it would never have crossed my mind to become an expert in the work of a poet from the North of England! Bur Ricks said, that's it, that's what you're doing. All of Bunting's books were out of print at the time, and I really thought Christopher was crazy. But he was percipient, absolutely right: Bunting wasn't much on the radar at the time, but he sure is now. It was a great project to make a critical edition of the poems, now published by Faber; and I'm already working on Bunting's selected prose for Flood Editions, who published my *Bunting's Persia*. Basil was way ahead of his time, and way out of it, too. His devotion to the regional and tradition fuelled in him an unprecedented modernism, even post-modernism, that only now is fully being recognized. His time has come, given his devotion to regional cultures, Persian and Arabic poetry, the politics of poverty, and much else besides. Every day his work seems richer and more prescient to me; the best poets are proleptic and odd, and that Basil.

You have won several awards, some for translation. Tell us what draws you to the art of translation.

For me, translation, like criticism, is a vital function of poetry. A translated poem is, of course, a poem, but one with a great responsibility - it has to convey things about another language and culture, perhaps even of another time. When I started to translate poetry, I was encouraged by Derek Walcott, luckily for me, who praised my Miguel Hernández book by saying that in my translations there was a "sense of shared elation between reader and translator that confirms the delight of exact sensation when the poem feels transmitted by that cautious and subtle alchemy that is the translator's skill." I'm fortunate to have received praise that actually defines what translation is, and that's delight, and sensation, and alchemy.

If you're interested in the translation of poetry, one thing you hear over and over and over again is that Octavio Paz said that all texts could be thought of as "translations of translations of translations." He must have written that in Spanish, of course; but what we get in English is this:

On the one hand, the world is presented to us as a collection of similarities; on the other, as a growing heap of texts, each slightly different from the one that came before it: translations of translations of translations.

123

So we stand on the shoulders of poetry giants from all languages. And I had great teachers, in translation: Rosanna Warren and William Arrowsmith. Rosanna was my mentor in all things relating to translation and editing; I'd not have translated Hernández, or learned how literary magazines work, except for her guidance over a great many years. As for Arrowsmith, I was one of his very last students, in graduate school. He had to stop teaching in the middle of the semester in which I was taking his brilliant class, "T. S. Eliot and the Mind of Europe." Out of breath and desperately thirsty, fumbling repeatedly for a plastic water bottle he carried with him in an old blue flight bag, Arrowsmith - tremendously ill - smiled as if teaching literature could make no man happier.

Arrowsmith suffered no fools and was intimidating; he could be blunt, and was always sharp. But I hung on his every word, little knowing that his words were, sadly, in very limited supply. Early in the semester, I gathered up enough nerve to go see him in his office. He'd put some material for the course on reserve in the library, and when I went to retrieve them I found things that were all in German, French, and Italian. I shuffled around the library shelves for the English versions; there were none. When I mentioned this to Arrowsmith he looked amazed. "You have to read them in the original," he said flatly. Unless, he proposed, I wasn't up to it. The hair on the back of my neck bristled: it was an eerie moment, as if all the greatest writers were staring at me. Once before, when I was in college, I had made the same mistake. A comp lit professor sent me off to read some Wagner, and though I had taken just enough German to read it, I found myself wanting to get by with some English versions. "Why?" the prof asked me - "it's beautiful in the German." Yet Arrowsmith did not dismiss me as a lazy or ignorant neer-do-well which, in fact, I was. He simply pointed out that yes, these works were beautiful in the original, and that as we were talking about the likes of Dante and Montale, it could scarcely be too much trouble to do as much work as they had, if I'd an honest interest in poetry.

He wasn't being pedantic. I don't know when it was that poets decided they didn't need to know as much as, say, Dante or Eliot ("The best method is to be very intelligent"), that we could skate by on nothing more than our own vocabularies and experience, translations occasionally in hand. My mentors sternly and generously sent me packing off to work harder, and I never have been able to thank them all enough.

I enjoyed reading Wishbone immensely; I appreciate its compressed and elegantly musical language. Are you a musician too?

Nobody's ever asked me that before. Yes! I taught myself how to play guitar and piano as a teenager, and played in homegrown bands in Memphis. I wrote songs by the guitar case full, and loved composing lyrics that went with the music. But I didn't have the charisma, if that's what it takes, to front a band. Also, I was too bookish, and looked it! So I drifted more and more toward the lyrics, and from there deeply into poetry itself. It felt natural, inevitable. Music was my first love, but poetry and I got married.

I like that! After *Wishbone*, I moved on to *Squandermania* which takes off in an entirely different direction. Can you expound on this?

Well, that book came before *Wishbone*, and had mostly to do with life around the time of 9/11, which is when I was working on it. Everything and everyone was under stress, and the language was under stress. We were learning just how lethal words are (how had we forgotten?). I'd turned to Hopkins and, you could say, got sprung; it was connected with what he called "the in-earnestness of speech." Anyway, it was my second book, and second books are always a problem, no? You don't want to repeat what you did in the first, but it's hard to know just how to move on, to move forward. That's my orphan book, *Squandermania*. I feel sorry for the thing now - it was published in the UK by a publisher that stopped publishing poetry books, so it became quite invisible. Tom Sleigh quite liked it, and when I read poems from it, people ask about the book. So that's enough for me, and who knows, maybe its lostness is still worth something. Everyone should have a ghost book.

How did *Union* come into being?

It was my first book, so it summed up what, till then, I could make out of a lifetime of experience growing up in Memphis, with all the music and terrible, fraught history that surrounded me. First books have a necessity and urgency about them. I could almost see the book fully formed before it existed. But a different person than I am now wrote those poems.

Please share with us how the connection between the Poetry Foundation and *Poetry* magazine has evolved over the years.

It's very simple: the magazine existed for 90 years before there was a Poetry Foundation. In 2003 on the surprise receipt of a major gift from the philanthropist and poet Ruth Lilly, the Poetry Foundation evolved from the Modern Poetry Association, which had been founded in 1941 to support the publication of *Poetry* magazine. Her gift made possible a building with a library and performance space for the public, our website at poetryfoundation.org, our collaboration with the NEA, Poetry Out Loud, and a variety of awards and fellowships for poets.

What exactly is the "Open Door" policy and how is it implemented?

The Open Door policy was devised by *Poetry's* founding editor, Harriet Monroe in 1912, and has been the (open) secret of our success and longevity. It says that "the editors hope to keep free of entangling alliances with any single class or school. They desire to print the best English verse which is being written today, regardless of where, by whom, or under what theory of art it is written." Whatever we do, each poem we read - and that's 150,000 submitted poems each year, read by the editors, not by interns, students, or outside readers - is contemplated with that vision firmly in mind; it's even inscribed on the wall here!

You are a celebrated editor, poet, translator, and scholar, so naturally reading and writing are intrinsic to both your professional and private life, but what do you do for fun with your non-literary friends?

I don't know about celebrated, but thank you for that adjective! You know, reading and writing and my work are what I do for fun. I'm afraid that's pretty much my whole life. I wish I could say I do something else, but then again, I wouldn't want to do anything else. As for friends, well, the amazing thing about poetry is that it brings you friends that you haven't even necessarily met in person. What richer kind of life is there? That said, Harriet Monroe was a mountain climber: she was an early proponent of the Sierra Club, knew John Muir, and actually died ascending Machu Picchu at the age of 75. So I have to remind myself to go outside one in a while, and do things to get away from the books and the submission system!

With the recent knowledge of proposed budget cuts to the NEA and other similar programs it seems like the future of poetry may be at risk. What measures must we take in order to protect the arts?

Well, so far, we've been able to stave off those cuts, thanks to the efforts everywhere of many citizens and groups and advocates for the arts. It will always be like this, and really, it always was. Vigilance is required; but in my heart I feel that the arts always find a way.

As an editor, what do you expect from a poem?

I expect a poem to defeat my expectations first and foremost, and to succeed on its own terms, if nothing else.

And lastly, it is always easier to be objective toward a work when you're wielding the editor's pencil, but as an author whom do you trust to provide unbiased feedback? If Don Share, the poet, were to submit a poem to *Poetry* magazine would you accept it?

One can't be objective or unbiased (is that even possible?) but I can be capacious and eclectic, as the Open Door policy obliges me to be, and as is my inclination, anyway. I defy anyone to tell what I like or don't like on the basis of what's in the magazine for the simple reason that it's not my job to publish what I like; a magazine based on what Don likes would not be a good premise for a magazine! I publish what I believe to best for our readers, and for the stewardship of our history; I try to do, as my eleven predecessors have, the work of discovery; it leads one into uncharted territory. When Harriet first read Eliot, Williams, Crane - what must it have seemed like? Poetry like theirs had never been read before. Anyway, I only had a poem in *Poetry* once, for whatever that's worth, under Joe Parisi; and all I can say now is that if Don Share were to submit work again to the magazine, he could not be on its staff, so that's that, for the time being! To more or less answer the question, let me end with what Patrick Kavanagh said: "I would not object if some critic said I wasn't a poet at all." As he put it, there was a kink in me, put there by Verse. So no feedback can save me, I'm afraid. "A man (I am thinking of myself) innocently dabbles in words and rhymes and finds that it is his life."

REVIEWS

Ambushing Water
by Danielle Hanson

Reviewed by Elizabeth Nichols

Danielle Hanson's *Ambushing Water* crashes into the senses like a wave into the earth. Hanson's language is crystal sharp and her imagery sparks off of the page like the glittering glare of the sun in still water. *Ambushing Water* shows the reader "the beautiful distortions of the earth" in each poem. The familiar sight of a bird—a recurring image throughout Hanson's collection—transforms into a "French Recipe," a painting, and "a tulip." Through the eyes of the speaker in Hanson's poems, the reader sees the world changed, as if she is looking at its image in an undulating pool. In the end, *Ambushing Water* lets the reader see the world through a poet's eyes and the reader is left reverent and awed.

The aforementioned recurring image of the bird in Hanson's collection serves to underscore the theme of transformation in the collection. In "Bird," the speaker describes a bird that is "almost touched / by shadow and begins / to close up a like a tulip," ultimately dissolving into "a vague black perfume." In "The Man is Walking His Bird on a Leash," the bird itself does not transform but instead transforms the world. The poem plays out like a chapter from a magical realism novel as the bird "once pulled so hard" on her harness that "she tore a hole through the air," leaving her owner no choice but to duct tape the hole in the air. In the last line, the reader learns that the bird "constantly dreams of the other side of the sky." Moreover, in "The Bird as a Painting," the image of the bird reduces the world into a two-dimensional space. The everyday occurrence of a bird running into a window becomes instead a work of art: a painting. Finally, in "He Beat Her," a scene of domestic violence is conveyed with the image of a bird. The image of the bird transforms the woman's body and stresses the horror that the woman is going through:

He Beat Her

>   And her back fell open
>   like a moth finding its wings.
>   He beat her and her back flew
>   open like a bird rising.
>   He beat her and her back
>   flew to a tree—
>   a tree was sketched
>   by the markings on her back.
>   He beat her and her back left
>   running so hard
>   it left its feet behind.

As suggested by "He Beat Her," Hanson's imagery imparts an eerie, unsettling beauty to difficult subject matter. In "Red Nail Polish," for example, Hanson describes the inner turmoil of a woman forced to change herself for another. "You asked me to paint my nails red," begins the speaker, "and so, of course, I did / even though I hated the way / they stalked the eye." The forced physical change causes the reader to disassociate from herself, transforming her hand into a sexualized object: "My hand was suddenly not my own. / It was five cherry bombs / waiting to go off. / My arm was the shadow / of a red light district." The speaker then feels repulsed at her own appendage: "I wanted to cut my fingers off, escape / but that would only let the color run / to the counter, the floor, / multiply like cockroaches and hide in the dark." In the last two lines, the speaker realizes that she cannot sever her grossly transformed hand. Just as she cannot sever her connection to the person that made her change herself—that transformed her until she could no longer see her self.

In fact, the transformation of the self—for good or bad—is one of the most potent themes in Ambushing Water. A particularly unique and powerful example of this is in the poem "Burial." In "Burial," the speaker describes a strange merging of souls, of selves:

Burial

> When Uncle was buried,
>> it was on top of Great-Grandfather
>>> for the cemetery had long been full on the ground
>>>> floor.
>
> Uncle was able to meet Great-Grandfather
>> for the first time since he was seven.
>>> Uncle was surprised by Great-Grandfather's
>>>> gingham dress,
>
> which, Great-Grandfather explained, was Cousin's.
>> Being buried next to each other, they had
>>> mixed together during their melting period.
>
> They were looking forward to what Uncle would bring.
>> Would he ante up a new toe for the ones that were lost?
>>> (Such is the absent-mindedness of the dead.)
> Great-Grandfather/Cousin also needed a belt
>> and memories of a colorful bird in a green, green tree.
>>> They wanted again to see what the eyes see as they
>>>> rot away,
> the beautiful distortions of the earth.

Here, death transforms the soul. Great-Grandfather appears to Uncle wearing Cousin's "gingham dress" because they Great-Grandfather and Cousin were buried next to each other. Moreover, at the end of the poem, Great-Grandfather and Cousin are named as one being, Grand-Father/Cousin, signaling that they are now one and the same. Their selves have merged. The proximity of the body, even in death, affects change in both parties, stirring something within. And, once again, the image of the bird returns. This time as a memory of Grand-Father/Cousin. In death, in this strange afterlife with melded souls, Grandfather/Cousin wants a bird's eye view of the world: "to see what the eyes see as they / rot away, / the beautiful distortions of the earth." The last lines are actually the speaker describing the last moments of the soul in death with the dying man's life flashing before his eyes. At the conclusion of life, then (just as in Hanson's collection), the world appears to the soul as a poem: as a beautiful distortion. Conclusively, Hanson's *Ambushing Water* allows the reader to see the world as the dying man, as the poet, sees it. The world is changed, changed utterly—beautiful, terrifying, poetical.

Equilibrium
by Tiana Clark

Reviewed by Linda Kim

Two halves of a whole, diametrically opposed, come together into gorgeous balance in Tiana Clark's *Equilibrium*. Beautiful and meditative, yet also fearlessly blunt, Clark's poetry strings together a stunning series of discoveries that form a cohesive narrative whole. The organization of her book is exquisite, with each poetic theme flowing into the next in a seamless latticework of artful craft. The elegant weaving of lineation carries a transformation of metaphor, allusions, and imagery. The next image, the next poem, the sum of all parts have been imbued with greater meaning. Her words are powerful to the point of gasping and being in want of breath; twists and turns of her meaning astound and resonate. *Equilibrium* is about bringing two halves of a whole into harmony, yet how is this possible when those two sides are in direct opposition while swallowed up by hatred?

How do you reconcile being the daughter and product of hateful marriage with the very human fear of whether you can be loved?

> Black Mom, wanting so badly
> to be consumed by a white man,
> for a white man to make her French
> toast from the inside-out.
>
> Their differences smashing into each other,
> skin engines of self-hatred that made me.

How does a black poet subvert the dehumanization of being the Other when simply asserting the right to exist is a political act in of itself?

> *She was caught between two allegiances, different,*

yet the same. Herself. Her race. Race! The thing
that bound and suffocated her. Whatever steps
she took, or if she took none at all,
something would be crushed. Crushed?

When one's identity exists in interracial liminality and is constantly underscored by the legacy of slavery, simply telling your own story requires the agency of courage. Yet Clark does so fearlessly. She charts out the raw and potent paths of racial politics. She navigates the sticky paradox of how to accept the Self while enduring the psychological landscape of being the Other. The struggle of carving out a space for yourself in the racial tapestry of America is difficult precisely when one doesn't fit in constrictive, narrow frames.

"Crack the interracial craving," she says, "before it cracks you."

Equilibrium opens with the poem "Equilibrium." As one title overlaps with the other, this yearning for harmony compounds itself. It is a thesis of the Self, the cold opening of an episodic glimpse into an unknown psyche. But the picture that quickly unveils and unfolds itself isn't a sketch of victimhood, not when the first lines of the first poem opens with, "Took me thirty years to say / I'm glad I don't pass for white."

Repetition is powerful. The poet uses it in other ways. "Mixed Bitch is allowed to love herself. / Mixed Bitch lets herself love— / the black inside: the white inside: the black of herself."

In arguing for the validity of her existence, for the humanizing need for love, she exemplifies the great truth of poetry: there is catharsis in storytelling.

Clark is a survivor. Self-portraits require a certain amount of vulnerability in order to be true, but the poet invites and accepts such scrutiny. In the act of speaking, she names her fear and takes control of it. Here, she explores the fragility of youth and childhood because family is as nurturing as it is damaging. There is tension in loving a mother who is both so sacrificial and yet so full of disapproval. There is tension in loving and hating an earthly father who is as absent as the heavenly one. The latter is a damning conflation that underscores every scene of Baptist religiosity with numb apathy; every invocation of the Father ultimately collapses under the excruciating weight of shame.

To be a young woman is to be an object of sex, a caricature of lust, a reduction of humanity. To be a sexual creature is to be condemned like when the speaker observes an exorcism performed in a church:

> But I knew this
> girl that twitched on the floor. Sarah, my older friend.
> And yes, she made out with boys. And yes, I saw
> how the boys looked at her breasts, like the way
> they looked at them now when she jiggled, buoyant
> as sunny side up eggs. As if I could pierce her yolks
> with my praying fingers, bloodletting buttery sex.
> She was like me: a girl with no father, a girl that
> made God her father, a girl that wanted to be saved,
> but mostly to be loved.

In learning to love herself and finding the worth of her existence, the poet has to grapple with religion and worship. But ritual, artifice, and constructions pale in the face of true simple belief. "How we fake to feel the magic inside us. It took me a while to understand / that I didn't have to beg for it. God was already washing the dust off my feet."

Beauty is fragile in existence. She "came into this world, creamy—full of alkali and burn, / like a baby born of hard labor." She came into a world that crucified her blackness as being tainted and unclean, where the assumption of strangers is that whiteness is automatically equated with clean. Merely having the sin of sexuality engenders body-shaming and violations of the self, as when charitable white church women invade her mother's home to clean the filth, poverty, and blackness away:

> One lady came out with my stained underwear, holding it up and away
> from her body like a stench. My period bruising the pearly cotton with
> a smear of red poppies. My horror, my ooze, my face—
>
>   I was the adulteress caught
> naked in the streets in front of Jesus. Their unsmiling, stone faces
> seeing my midras, my unclean spot before them.
> The way they slashed their guillotine eyes at my fresh body—
> to have had so much blood in me like a dirty, new sin.

Yet no matter how destructive it is to internalize shame, there is nothing quite as painful as the act of self-destruction. "You made kinky your nemesis, fought / genetic bend of curls." In the pursuit of American ideals of beauty, the speaker gives herself over to physical mutilation and psychological self-harm. She straightens her "burnt black hair" with "matchsticks ignited on the scalp."

But physical agony doesn't compare to the sheer emotional anguish every time she makes the decision to ignore the pain, to instead "suck it up, keep it in, tucked and folded / like origami." Yet no matter how hard she tries to punish her curls, it would never swing like a white girl's hair. Instead, whenever "the teeth / of a hot comb forged from the European Gods of smooth metal" is taken to her scalp, it breaks her wavy locks "like the back / of a slave into submission, into black yarn I knew inside me grew / to find my way out of this chemical labyrinth."

Crinkled hair is to be as mastered just as much as the body is to be tamed. She yearns to break free from the prison of her own making. The comb may as well be modern shackles for all that it is used as a tool of conformity and shame. And yet the comb is still tempting. Its influence is that insidious. It's as difficult to put down as easy it is to get lost in a maze. Clark is as concerned with the history of slavery as she is with the black image in America. Internalizing worthlessness creates a pattern of behavior that is hard to avert, but what's even harder to confront is your own "Minotaur of self-hatred," to slay that "beast of pretty!"

Skin is a cage that is distressingly easy to slip into whenever the poet is branded as a "nigger." It is a label laden with "molten syllables as searing lassos around my neck." It is the brand of a slave, a victim, an Other.

She says, "You never forget the first time / you are branded with iron— seared raw, permanent." Because once you are named as such you are nothing else. It sticks with you forever, searing your brain. Even after justice is wrought, the damage is already done.

The trauma is unending, as if on infinite loop. As it is when social media circulates sensationalized clips of slaughter on streets:

Praises for the video, to the witness & his recording thumb, praises to YouTube for taking the blindfold off Lady Justice, dipping her scales down with old weight

of strange fruit, to American eyeballs blinking & chewing the 24-hour news cycle: *another black body, another white cop.*

Images repeat. History repeats. The poet begins this lament of senseless death with, "A video looping like a dirge on repeat, my soul—a psalm of bullets in my back." She ends on a line that abruptly cuts off: "A video looping like a dirge on repeat—" Callback and repetition. There is nothing left after this but blank white space. Yet the greater overarching themes of the book quickly rush to fill in that empty space, transforming the silence instead into a yearning for harmony that compounds endlessly like an open ended question, an answer without end, an ontological debate as impenetrable as God's existence.

Eventually, finally, she can accept that "I came / into this world greasy, full of thick psalms. Let the water take me back."

Forty Miles North of Nowhere
by LeRoy N. Sorenson

Reviewed by Elizabeth Nichols

LeRoy N. Sorenson's *Forty Miles North of Nowhere* stirs up the dust of small American towns fallen on tough times, courting the specters of better days. His collection is at once a lament and an ode to small-town rural America, barren but ripe with golden memories. Sorenson's imagery hits the reader in the gut. He does not spare the reader the poverty, the alcoholism, the death, or the dreams lost in the rubble. Like an aching tooth that he cannot help but worry, Sorenson wonders at, and rues over, a past defined by loss and a present haunted by ghosts. Sorenson's timely collection takes the reader into a place that "Christian gods abandoned… / years ago:" a place that is forty miles north of nowhere, yet filled with a human experience that is rawer and more tender to the touch than anywhere else.

    Sorenson's collection is haunted at its core. Each section has its ghosts. Indeed, the speaker in the collection realizes in "Among the Survivors" that he "had no / idea how deep my haunting ran." The primary personas in *Forty Miles North of Nowhere*—father, mother, and townspeople—are also not aware how deeply they are haunted. In "Ghosts at Craigville," the speaker describes the ghosts of the past that fill a logging camp: "At night, phantoms climb / out of thin graves, make their way / to greener places." In "The Haunting of Verna's Farm," Verna's "door knocks at the oddest times" and "She flings it open to find her dead / husband, his hat in hand, / her love for him a lightning rod." And, in "This Was the Moment," the speaker's mother jerks away from him, "Fists clenched, quivering, / punching phantoms, eyes terrible / and mad." Forty miles north of nowhere, the living cannot escape the ghosts of their loved ones or the ghosts of their own making. The prominence of ghosts in Soresnon's collection makes Death as much of a character in this small American town as the speaker and his family.

There is one haunting in particular that casts a heavy shadow over the collection. At the beginning of the collection, "Brother" is the first of several poems that describe the death of the speaker's sibling. The poem sets the tone for the rest of the collection, signaling to the reader that there is a gloom that seeps into every space of this small-town, USA. "Sometimes," admits the speaker in the first stanza, "I stand / in front of your grave, / imagine your fingers / grabbing my ankles / for solace, seeking escape." It is striking that the reader is directly addressed as "you," essentially cast as the deceased in a one-sided conversation between the speaker and his brother's ghost. With rich, dark imagery, the reader learns that the brother died premature as a very young child: "Head swollen, small / mewling sounds, your / fingers slipping through / our mother's fingers…." In the end, the speaker sees his brother turn to him "clear of body, restraint / and smile," and knows that "You were a part / of me given unto death." The last line suggests that even if the speaker were to leave his small town forty miles north of nowhere, part of him would never leave.

As the ghosts also suggest, Sorenson presents the reader with the full human experience—with whole lives born, lived, and died in a single poem. Such is the case with the poem "A Thousand Acres Faded Yellow." Throughout, Sorenson carefully crafts poignant images to reveal the spoken and unspoken in the lives of an old married couple:

A Thousand Acres Faded Yellow

>
> The old man and woman cling to their house,
> their days limp from his rage, her sorrow.
> Geese and chicken strut in the yard and wolves
> circle closer every day. They keep
> the riffraff away. The days offer the same old
> insult, the nights' ghosts shimmering on
> prairie's edge. Sprouted wheat the sure sign
> of decay. What is killing them is memory
> and hope. The woman sees their children
> romp from the barn, screaming in delight
> and the old man lives in the days
> when he tossed hay bales twenty feet.
> They will not visit their dead
> at the Mennonite church. If belief
> is strong enough, the dead are wiped away

> and the children return. Neighbors bring
> crude bread and sweet apple pie
> and the men sneak a bottle of corn to ease
> the pain. At summer's end, failing
> to summon mercy and white clouds,
> the couple dies in final denial. The wolves
> enter the yard. The trees turn fire red.

Here, Sorenson sets up contrasting images to facilitate a sense of unease. The reader is given the traditionally wholesome and warm images of children romping and "sweet apple pie," but then must set them against wolves circling and fire red trees. Once again, ghosts haunt the poem, "shimmering on the prairie's edge" and in the memories of the old man and woman. The key line in the poem—"What is killing them is memory and hope—" at once illustrates the physical and emotional decay that will be the death of the old couple. The poem ends like a parable with the old man and woman dying in denial, and the wolves entering the yard. In the end, the old couple do not escape the small town, and instead become a part of the crowd of ghosts that possess the town and its living.

Silence also reigns in Sorenson's collection. There is the silence of a town bereft of the humming of its industry from its golden days. There is the "silence of the meadow," "of secrecy," "the silence of witness," and the "silence of the grave." Even language is paradoxically rooted in silence. In "The First Sad Man I Knew," the speaker's father sings to a stripped sky, "his words born from silence." In fact, there is a "Lexicon of silence," filled with the empty word of the departed.

Or, in the case of "Prairie Bed," the soon-to-be-departed. Here, the reader learns that *Forty Miles North of Nowhere* is not just a physical place. It is a state of mind, and tragic way of living. In "Prairie Bed," the speaker wrestles with the impending death of his father. Driving down a seemingly endless stretch of road, cattle dotting the landscape, the speaker and his father are momentarily trapped in a nowhere-state. In a limbo between life and death. Everything is ashy, gray. Hazy. There is a deep-seated feeling of unreality. The road's ribs evoke the skeletal thinness that cancer and chemo treatment can cause. The father's dry cough punctuates and stresses the silence that pulls at the speaker's soul:

Prairie Bed

He jerked away, spurted in anger: *Don't.*

I wheeled him into a room of tubes
and drip bags, a barber's chair. The intercom
above crackled mumbles, his skin a dry
Parchment. I put my hand on his.

We had driven into Minnehaha County, home
of the chemo center—a building of soft
murmur, killing drugs. He had a dry cough.
The cool air shivered me, sweat spots spread
under his armpits—the walls an orange pink.

Driven side-by-side into sun, the tinted
windshield turning everything ashy,
the car's engine humming the freedom
of speed, cattle blurring in the side
Windows. He had a dry cough.

Driven on country tarmac,
crooked white lines stretching
into hazy glare, tires thumping
over the road's ribs, a decade-long
silence between us like a stubborn stain.

In the end, the speaker is left with a single word: *Don't.* After being a passenger in a car full of stressed silence—after going on this journey to *Forty Miles North of Nowhere*—with the speaker and Sorenson, the reader cannot help but wonder why anyone would return. The answer lies in the collection's final poem, "Schooled." In spite of the dust and decay, the ever-present ghosts and death, the speaker still holds onto sweet memories. Memories that are perhaps sweeter for their juxtaposition to the darkness of his small town. Alongside the horror, he remembers "Mrs. Jensen" and "her creamy / face and small condolences," and Arthur Miller with his "yellow teeth." Even though the speaker's final thought is that "The best hope" is "twenty / miles down the only road, / pedal to the floor," he cannot leave this town and its people behind, because it is an integral part of him. If he left it behind, if he gave up its ghost, he would lose himself. For, in the end, that is what *Forty Miles North of Nowhere* is: a presentation of the speaker's most inner, inextricable self.

Riding Thermals to Winter Grounds
by Djelloul Marbrook

Reviewed by Linda Kim

In Djelloul Marbrook's *Riding Thermals to Winter Grounds* the poet goes through a series of identity metamorphoses. Overcome with "bewilderness" and "doubtfulness," while in distress over the state of the world, his speakers invariably echo his cynical sentiments about life and growing up. His thematic concerns inject anxiety into his poems. He is endlessly preoccupied with death and decay, faces and nakedness, skewed perspectives, societal disillusionment, invisibility in urbanity, and finally the intangibility of the Self. In this chaotic world one must endure "loudmouths & exhibitionists" and the sheer overwhelming quality of loneliness. Even when surrounded the poet is alone. In such circumstances what can "we use to get our bearings?"

>Faces that threaten to disappear,
>promise, threaten, seem likely
>to disappear, are Lenten roses;
>I am the snow they drink.
>Nothing can be done for them
>but adoration and resolve
>not to gather them in love
>or fear.
>   Who is the poison,
>seer or seen, the pale rose
>or one who leaves footprints
>in the snow?
>
>   I looked back
>as a child and noticed
>I left no footprints anywhere.

This is a world in which "the gray parents whose fumbling inside / led to my urgent mistake, a life / of unwantedness, a misdemeanor."

A world in which exists venomous "despair / so pure there is no antidote."

The conviction of being unwanted haunts all of Marbrook's poems. His speakers embody "the lone survivor / of a cataclysmic embitterment, / the estrangement of...birth." His poetry is obsessed with understanding identities, shape, and form—be they physical or psychological. "Birthmark / borne from a savage place" is a source of both revulsion and also acute fascination. He is insatiable for answers and relentless in trying to discover what is "hidden."

Because in his eyes faces are compositions of artifice. "Ponds and fires and eyes of others, stare," bringing with it nothing but discomfort and social awkwardness. They epitomize the excruciating nature of being seen and trapped under scrutiny. The poet is similarly struck dumb with deafness, blindness, and speechlessness whenever a confused brain works to dampen and deconstruct the senses that would otherwise illuminate.

Social contact can be scarring. Relationships can end in lies. Pain is inevitable and evident in the "burnt imprint" of leaves "on the grass, a stain / on the sidewalk, a few mysterious cuttings, / a shadow that cannot be accounted for."

> As it is you have been like
> ink hanging in the air,
> a fume
> through which it's dangerous to walk.

In the estranged landscape of Marbrook's book, there is a distinct reluctance to engage with other human beings. It is all too easy to understand his inclination to withdraw entirely, to shy away from potential future hurts.

"Life is a crisis, a cry," he says, noting how unrelenting it is in its uncertainties. "There's no help for any of this / except our tendency to rot, / our insistence on being not." Helplessness blinds him when there is no agency. Regret is related to the eyes, gaze, body, and perception. But Marbrook's book advocates to penetrate that obfuscation with self-awareness and insight instead. There is agency in bearing witness to such suffering, and then learning to evolve beyond it. The yearning to permeate the world with a tangible proof of his existence manifests into a will to survive.

An existential need drives his poetry. He takes it as his sacred duty to be a scribe because in the act of witnessing is the assertion that he exists: "Witness this re-panic: / words leave their meanings behind." There is bravery in scrawling "in honest grit / the words I thought would be the death of me to say."

Even though "Each face is a garden / in a certain state of decay," there is still burgeoning hope "in that decay / the future is born and joy leans towards the sun." Despite resurgences of darkness, never-ending cycles, even death must eventually yield to rebirth and life.

Although spring flora must first fight to break free from the onset of winter decay and rot, they will eventually flourish in the sun. The Lenten roses and dandelions will come. After all, the Lenten rose is among the best perennials for shade.

Suites for the Modern Dancer
by Jill Khoury

Reviewed by Linda Kim

A body of work is a malleable space, poetry even more so. In Jill Khoury's *Suites for the Modern Dancer,* the body is a landscape on which to impart meaning, a table of "translucent skin / on which is inscribed / a topographical depiction." Objects imply meaning beyond the constraints of their physical forms. Subtext is spurred on the wings of implication while the space between enjambed words and white space creates alternative versions of truth. Consequently, rereading unlocks greater depths, with layers of subject matter unfolding on top of each other.

The body and its individual parts make for marvelous imagery, producing a roadwork that maps the neural network of a unique mind. Strings of startling juxtapositions reveal the myriad and imaginative ways poets and artists form mental associations. New meaning is created through the combinations of objects placed together out of context. By reassembling them together in new ways, the poet keeps us surprised. Like in any great classical painting, a carefully balanced composition is made, as evident in this collage: "We are sphere and feathers, / thorns, knotholes, electricity, fractured light."

A corpus is a collection of written work, but in anatomy it is also the main body or mass of a structure. The book is thus structured on the inner workings of mind and body, exploring the tension between interiority and exteriority. Oftentimes, that tension can take the form of two competing yet harmonious poetic forms entwined and braided together within the same poem. One narrative thread informs understanding upon the other. The discrepancy between what is actually happening in the narrative and what is actually occurring in the character's thoughts creates a rich psychological landscape, as evidenced in the disorientating and disjointed experience of drowning:

  Tidal pressure   lungs fill up
  Sand recedes   reveals my mother

  From the crib my   hands found paper orbs
  when the water pushes you down, relax
  I spun the moon   around the sun

  Sleep is to inhale   dive under   Dad says
  hold your breath   *your body will find its way*

  I have no trouble   carrying water in me

  Coral is actually   bone
  Chitinous mass   sucked by wet sand
  their nervous system is ladderlike

  Multiple forms are at work here. Spacing and lineation establishes a pattern of reality while italics weaved throughout signify a distinct interiority. Short terse phrases separated by space emulates the out of control crashing of tides, a rhythm of empty space and chaotic lines. But with every italicized word, every calming thought and fatherly advice, the speaker's instinctual panic is slowly released. In the long suspended moment of oxygen deprivation, the speaker imagines a surreal melding of human body and animal form in order to simulate safety. Stability is thus achieved with this transfiguration.

  The gorgeous lyrical verse of the book is not afraid to be experimental in order to perfectly encapsulate the experience of inner worlds. More poems exhibit this quality through enigmatic and elusive phrasings like "My jaw is liquid" and "My palm stiff, upturned, a convex shadow," which hint at more rich interiority hiding just beneath the surface.

  A keen awareness of physiology underpins the whole book, making the reader aware of flesh on a cellular level. Thicket and trees can transform into threads of nerves while the brain can transfigure from "an aberration, / an apparition, a mass, a manse, / a monster" into "Spirit corral." The primary speaker scrutinizes and examines corporeality in ways that can both inspire and unnerve. Such observations are made also acutely personal through her own interactions with her disability and cane, which is as stark white as bone.

Imagery and metaphor blends seamlessly, succinctly chosen diction contains dualities of meaning, and the body is a corpus that engenders metatextual understanding. Sometimes the poetry will slyly call attention to the art of craft by illuminating its own process of creation. At other times a poem will reinforce the idea that the body is a corpus of poetic forms, lyrical skins, and cerebral creations. Poems succeed when they ascribe complex abstract thoughts to concrete imagery, and the poet displays a deft grasp of form and the ways to dissect it.

But if the eyes, lips, and lungs can incite emotional stories that sting, this is even more so whenever the poet focuses on the soft fragility of skin, the only thing holding back blood:

> Spidery capillaries
> indicate service roads that trail off
> —no access. But further south they branch
> into rural routes, then avenues and highways.
> Clusters of bruise-colored towns.

Blood acts as the connective tissue between psychology and physiology, a precious fluid that is both a literal transport of life and a metaphorical repository of identity. Though its crimson color permeates the text and grips its protagonists tight, the dreamlike quality to the poetry makes one question the razor thin divides between dreams and memories, fiction and reality. Wrists are slit and skin gets bruised, but the surreality of the book otherwise softens these gut punch blows. And yet the question of what is real and what is false makes the ambiguity all the more insidious for it.

"In fever, I record time as dreams," says the speaker. The bending of time and perception alters memories. Oppressive chains of the past looms large in each character's psyche. Past trauma tricks and traps characters into falling back into old behavioral patterns even as they yearn to break free. Reconnecting with the past in healthy ways requires an acceptance of the Self, but it can be difficult. Family dissolution and absence sunders and fractures whole an earth in which nothing can grow. Trying to "make a garden sprout from Alabama clay" produces nothing but "dead maples wound with kudzu."

Yet it is possible to grow anew. The narrative follows women at different points in their lives as they re-examine and re-contextualize their significant traumas. Reality is perceived as a "watercolor Rorschach." Reshaping identity is a muddled, skewed, messy endeavor.

One woman admitted to a psychiatric ward is haunted by the color red, which has hunted her all her life like the specter of the murderers who killed her mother:

> Over the white pillow, a torrent
> of red curls. Emma's hair is red
>
> like strawberries and stop signs.
> Red like valentines. Red like mine.
>
> Emma calls it "redrum red,"
> like a bloodcurdling lipstick scream.

She had once overdosed on alcohol and pills only to be rescued by EMTs. "Emma chokes: / branch / in her throat / NG tube / drags / poison out." But in the actuality the poison she truly craves to carve out of her is the memory of her pain.

Latter after going through therapy she tries to lead others as well, only to feel a fraud. "On the outside: / support group leader. She writes on the whiteboard: *how to let go of / anger. Self-compassion.* Carnival smile is also Emma." The italics denote another reality in which Emma feels trapped by artifice, making this another example of rich interiority. Her struggle to put on a role that rings hollow parallels her struggle to reframe herself as a survivor instead of a victim. Memory may as well be in constant replay just like the "marathon about serial killers" that plays on TV; it betrays her fears. And yet determination seizes her daily. She can still see beauty. "Emma's camera catches shadows of crayfish, tiny and muscular, / the afterimage of fingerling salmon shimmering / through clear musical pools." There's merit to life. There's still hope.

Another woman has a similar realization. While contemplating "a push, a plunge, a falling" into a well, she leans "her torso on its edge, strokes the inner wall / slippery with moss, gravity, danger" and craves *"something primal."* The allure of non-existence is strong. But in imagining what if she were to actually fall in, she is instead overcome: "How Annie would claw her nails into the slick. / How, if someone found her, ten fingernails / would sport a green-black cap, down to the quick." Annie wishes to live.

Poems about regret and grief give way to the presence of death, but suicide and self-harm and rape are become contrasted with the human desire to live. The body is a collective landscape of scars and stories, but trauma can be healed. The broken pieces of personhood can be put back together again.

As these women come to revise their own understandings of reality, so do the readers reframe their understandings of these characters. Poetry has the ability to capture the fundamental truths and existential workings of the mind, revealing ways in which they reshape reality. To reclaim identity is to regain your voice. To believe in hope is a paradigm shift in identity. Not all changes are positive. Neither is a therapeutic journey always smooth. Regression is easy, with vulnerability an ever slippery slope. It's a constant battle to not break down or become a reduction of themselves, strangers in their own skin: "I itch. Sleeves and arms / sew a new skin."

But so long as one continues to fight, to cling to hope, there is always the chance for opportunity. Mere existence is not living, but it can transcend into something more. Love can be found. Fearful inhibitions can be shed. And rebellion is always a choice. When all inhibitions are let go and the characters can finally grow, the body dances without a hint of self-consciousness—just the joy of movement. They will break free with resiliency. Because even at their lowest point, these characters keep pushing at the boundaries of their constraints. They become more than ink on the page. They become "worthy to be anyone's / guide."

What Are We Not For
by Tommye Blount

Reviewed by Elizabeth Nichols

Tommye Blount's *What Are We Not For* is a transformative collection that explores the ways in which human bodies are cast as *other*, as outside the norm. Blount masterfully uses images of dogs, bugs, puppets, and werewolves to symbolize bodies that have been forcefully pushed out of a normative space out of fear and ignorance. In the opening poem of the collection, "Bareback Aubade with the Dog," the speaker describes a moment of anxiety and misunderstanding to the reader. The speaker is afraid of dogs and tenses as the dog's leash snaps. But the dog passes the speaker by and instead launches its body into the lake, lapping up water. A moment of fear unexpectedly turns into a moment of beauty with the dog's slim head bucking "twice more / against the water's vermillion ripple." The poem's key line underscores the speaker's error in jumping to the conclusion that the dog was violent: "With my eyes shut, / I braced for what comes to those afraid / of what they refuse to see." Instead of seeing the dog, the speaker only saw a violent attacker. In turn, instead of being seen as human bodies, the bodies in Blount's timely collection are seen as animalistic, as violent, as *other*. In *What Are We Not For,* the line between the *other*—the image of the dog—and the normative blur until the distinction is a stark, cruel injustice.

Blount does not shy away from horror. In fact, it is horror that helps bodies branded as *other* reclaim their humanity. In "The Lynching of Frank Embree," the speaker addresses the lynched body in five parts, trying to grapple with a murder that has become an exhibit in a museum. "I've come to watch like all the rest," the speaker tells the photograph of the lynched man. "They are watching me / watching you," he goes on, "But to watch means that you are still alive / and it's too late for that, isn't it? / Object: you have become an artifact: a thing I lean in or / away from. Thing. Thing. Thing. You are a thing. No, / your body is a sculpture made of skin, vein, and muscle." It is critical that the speaker addresses the lynched man as "you" because he is also directly addressing the reader. He is casting the reader as *other* just as the lynched man was cast as *other*. Moreover, the speaker struggles to view the image of the lynched man as a human being and not an object on display. He fights to see the pieces of a human body and not a thing, not an *other*. The line between the speaker and the image of the lynched man blurs in part two of the poem:

From The Lynching of Frank Embree

> ...Your mouth It's black and big It's a mouth
>
> connected to an even blacker body Black nigger they say and I reach for my body
>
> dark and big as history Our bodies are museums
> Our bodies are objects in a museum A thing a thing

This blurring between the speaker and the lynched man becomes non-existent as the speaker describes the physical sensation that the lynched man experienced: "Falling over my eyes, a dark hood." Note that even the stanzas in in part two are devoid of punctuation, underscoring the sensation of a joining between the speaker and the lynched man—between the present and history. The speaker recognizes that his black body is also *other:* it is also an object in this museum with people looking at him as he looks at the lynched man. With no barrier left between them, the speaker's conflicting emotions surface: "I'm afraid of your big black body, / so I too worship it when I mean to / destroy it. By "it" I'm speaking of my body too. / You with the dumb look of hope. How / dare you look at me that way? / As if I have come to save you." The speaker's recognition of his own body as *other* turns to outrage and then to anger. He lashes out: "This is all your fault. You should have run faster." The speaker's complicated emotions stress the unnatural horror of the act of lynching and the unnatural, cruel act of labeling another being as an object, as *other*.

Finally, in the titular poem of the collection, "What Are We Not For," Blount uses metaphor to describe how it feels to live as *other*. The speaker asks, "What Are We Not For / but to be broken / like the deer resting on the side of the highway, in a bed made of / its insides? Isn't the scene always / the same—the rump and the legs / frozen in its last kick?" Here, Blount's lines are potently timely, tapping in director Jordan Peele's 2017 horror film *Get Out,* which not only features a scene with a car-struck deer, but also brings the issue of the envy and coveting of black bodies and culture front and center. Once again, the speaker's body is likened to an animal's, treated as not even human. The speaker says *other* bodies are meant to be broken, and are meant to blamed. He says, "I have too have lost my gaze, / the grip of the wheel— / like the one that plowed into / the deer. Wheel, will—it's all the same. And the ear does fail me at times, / as it must have the deer / that should have listened better." In other words, the deer is supposedly responsible for its own death. It should have seen the car coming. This false, criminalizing line of thinking is also applied to the *other* who is blamed for violence perpetrated against him for simply being different. "After all," the speaker concludes, "I am a broken animal. I am brokered in the name of the wheel." What the speaker is not for is to be an animal, to be made an *other* by those in control of the wheel. To be blunt, Blount's collection describes the current state of race relations in the United States. The bodies of *others* are being left on the side of the road like so many wounded deer. They are being treated as objects, as not-human. Blount's *What Are We Not For* calls out this injustice, using poetry as the medium to reclaim the humanity of the *other*.

The Wire Fence Holding Back the World
by Martin Willitts Jr.

Reviewed by Elizabeth Nichols

Martin Willitts Jr.'s *The Wire Fence Holding Back the World* taps into the philosophical and literary world of the Sublime. Like the man in Caspar David Friedrich's famous Romantic painting Wanderer above the Sea of Fog, the reader stands with Willitts Jr. on a poetic precipe, awestruck at the majesty and beauty of the natural world. With lyricism and rich imagery, Willitts Jr. follows in the footsteps of Romantic poets like Wordsworth and Coleridge as he sheds light on the unfathomable greatness of life. Each poem presents a facet of awesome nature, such as "Landslide," "Bumble Bees," "Barn Swallows," "Storm," "Rain," "*Autumn Clouds,*" and Winter Solstice." Even in darkness, in ugliness, Willetts Jr. still finds hope—hope illuminated by poetry. Willitts Jr. urges the reader to step beyond the wire fence holding him back from the world. He urges the reader to see a lighted world, to see "How nothing is the same when we find the Sublime."

In the titular poem of the collection, Willitts Jr. lays out his poetic prescription for the reader. His imagery paints a world beyond a barbed wire fence awash with light and life. The speaker in the poem watches as "birds crash through sunbreak" and wonders what he has achieved that could match the beauty of the scene before him. The speaker's awe-inspired question is right in line with the original definition of awe as a mix of fear and wonder, which is what the Romantics' stressed that the Sublime should inspire. In the end, the speaker cuts the wire fence holding the world back from him, and in doing so suggests to that the reader must also cut the fence that holds him back.

From "The Wire Fence Holding Back the World"

> Light ripples at sunrise
> against large dark chunks of breaking night
> and the moon folds behind blistered skies
> lit by coat-ember light.
>
> ...
>
> Here is where I dig in—
> spade breaking soil in intermittent rain
> And sun, between gasp and fear,
> Before this world goes all the way to forgetfulness.
>
> ...
>
> ...Here light comes—
>
> down the hills, touching every leaf
> making them hum. My face feels sun
> As the ground deepens brown, finds tree stumps,
> And voles slinking in wet, uncut grass.
>
> I grip hard on this world. I won't let go—
> although, a faraway voice calls to me,
> I make the hard decision to stay. Here
> light shocks. I cut a barbed wire fence.

Willitts Jr.'s treatment of the Sublime is not all idyllic. In "As Much As Some People Try to Destroy the Earth and All of Its Inhabitants, There is Still Some Small Hope," the speaker acknowledges that there men who are putting up fences instead of cutting them down, trying "to eradicate all wildness." Unlike the speaker, the "few in power" do not "approach the mysterious as a lover does—" as a quintessential Romantic does. Instead, the "few in power" are alienated from wildness, ignorant of the fragile connections they destroy:

From *As Much As Some People Try to Destroy the Earth and All of Its Inhabitants, There is Still Some Small Hope*

> As the few in power try to eradicate all wildness,
> they do not notice the deep well
> of interconnected and interdependent species
> and how it might lead to their eventual downfall eventually,
> and how it is an increasing countdown.
>
> There is such a thing as too much timid caution—
> it's not good for you. In this high heat, shadows undulate
> and flow, like blue honeysuckle on vines. Time
> has its own pace as if it was a whisper of tomorrow.
> It does not do any good to be impatient for stars to appear.
> Soon there will be too many to count.

The hope offered in the last stanza is subtle. The speaker reminds the reader that Time has its own pace—that the reader cannot stop its inevitable march. Nor can the reader stop the entirety of what the "few in power" have set in motion. Yet, the speaker reveals, all is not lost. In the creeping shadows of destruction, there is light. The speaker lets the reader know that soon, in the midst of shadow, there will be countless little lights, buoying hope.

In fact, Willits Jr. leaves the reader filled with light. Having sharpened his shears on each poem, the reader comes to the end of the chapbook ready to cut the wire fence holding him back. He has felt the awesome majesty of nature through Willits Jr.'s lyric, imagery-rich poems. He has heard the "Song" of a meadowlark, flickering like "wavering candlelight," and smelled the "Hedgerow Rose," "kissing" like hundreds of red petals on [his] neck." With the guidance of the speaker, the reader has faced "Extreme Heat," and braved "This Hard Winter." And now, at the end of this Sublime collection, the reader is ready to cut the wire fence holding him back—to know "if light is in every place, every tree sap, / every river resolved to be better, every / traveler resting on the roadside." In other words, the reader is ready to know if the world is Sublime beyond the sharp, cutting wire fence:

Inside Everywhere There Is Light
"And we can't see it but we think there's a light inside /
Everything," — William Stafford, Report to Someone

There will be a day
when we won't be able to explain anything—

an interval of light from the junipers;
a red aura of a cliff; flecks
of hair on our wrist
finding a pattern of lilac from a cold sun;
The miniature lives owned by rust—

Find that intimate glare before it's too late,
tell me what it looks like:
does it glow over tracts of land; or
does it recede and hide? I have to know
if light is in every place, every tree sap,
every river resolved to be better, every
traveler resting on the roadside
holding a sign telling us where he wants to go
knowing we will never take him all the way.

Every hand letting go of a seed
and the seed itself is light; outside
that last light of day peers over the edge
to see where it is going next.

 Here, the speaker describes light touching everything, and existing even within the tiniest seed. Light seeps into life, and pours from within it, peering "over the edge." In the last stanza, one can see the as he reader leans over the edge with speaker, and looks at the light leading him into the distance. Nature, imbued with the Sublime, has lead the reader to hope. With Willits Jr.'s collection, it is as if the reader has picked up the shears to cut his wire fence. As he holds the chapbook in his hands, he has the world poetically presented to him, painted in the image of the Sublime. With *The Wire Fence Holding Back the World* in his hands, the reader sees the world lighted, the world Sublime, the world changed.

Woman in a Blue Robe
by Yoko Danno

Reviewed by Linda Kim

With quiet moments of life captured in lyrical verse, Yoko Danno's *Woman in a Blue Robe* showcases a keen awareness of natural beauty. This is especially so when offset against the aftermath of atomic destruction, historic acts of war, or geological acts of God. But even when injustices are wrought, the poet doesn't react to life with bitterness. Instead, she exudes a philosophical calm. Consequently, her poems are contemplative and meditative. Buddhist iconography lends itself well to a text that approaches life and its disasters with a distinct acceptance. This is crucial because central to the theme is the great question of identity.

In the poem, "Germination," even the title pushes forward this thematic tension. Of her mother, the poet asks:

> Where was I
> before I was inside you?
>
> Was I blowing
> like a wind across the sky,
> slipping through a cloud of birds?
>
> You were there in the seed, dear
>
> *Is that why I was named Yoko, 'Leaf-Child'?*

The desire to know the meaning behind one's name reveals the universal human desire to understand one's place. Because once identity is established, peace can be achieved.

How the speaker finds this peace within her existence is found in the rest of the poem, which shifts its focus to a specific moment: "A welcome rain / falls on the mountains / changes into / quick-crystal streams, / glancing through rocks." This instance of natural beauty eventually culminates into an archetype of Mother Earth embracing the transformation as "growing and glowing, sweet."

Thus, the biological mother who birthed the speaker has now become ambiguously melded with a Gaia figure; the earth itself takes on the shape of a womb. This speaks to the close affinity the speaker shares with nature, as if it is only right that humanity be intrinsically rooted in a mutual respect for life. This poem, among many others, argues for the validity and continuity of a natural world, which we must protect.

In the process, she asserts that all life is precious. Culture is sacred. Danno's poetry cherishes the ancient traditions and histories of Japan. They have clearly influenced her. She wears her literary inspirations proudly, with her allusions ranging from Emily Dickinson and Greek mythology to Saigyō and Bashō. These allusions contribute to the almost mythic feel of the storytelling style she takes on to tackle the scope and scale of the Japanese folklore she admires.

The worth of keeping alive the zeitgeist of ancient Japan is made especially apparent when the poetry exalts in Bashō's impact on the literary world. The way Danno observes the natural world is similarly as beautiful and pensive as his:

> sunlit maple trees burst into red and yellow
> preparing for loneliness in deep snow
> and the approach of silence below zero

Her poetry retains this haiku-like pinpoint focus on flora, fauna, and minimalist imagery throughout the book. But of all the seasonal moments she ponders over, this stanza in particular captures the glorious spirit of change. Its kinetic energy is fluid in how it transitions from autumn's celebratory end to the quieter and slower pace of winter. Her perception of the world is acute: there is still joy to be found in life even when joy is fleeting in the face of death. Yet there is still "consolation in solitude."

Life is outside of our control. The only things that can be controlled are our reactions to the world. Identity is determined by the pattern of actions an individual takes. Peace within yourself comes from self-awareness. Until then it is the poet's job to keep interrogating self-identity.

In searching for answers, Danno displays a deft directorial sense of light, as when she crafts anticipation and a sense of discovery:

> A black swallowtail fluttering
>   from a mist of orange blossoms
> leads me to an empty hallway:
>   through a crack in the closed door
> a shaft of sunlight pierces the dark.

There are always questions to be asked, brought to light, and illuminated upon with answers. She exhibits an Imagist sensibility in when and how enigmatic images are chosen to be shown. This tendency reveals much about the way her mind works.

"You have to go through life, door- / to-door, looking for hidden answers."

In service to this exploratory spirit, the lineation of her poetry is concise and clever. Danno's verse is as free form and elegant as it needs to be and is cohesive in both its minimalistic aesthetic and the way it handles light. Hidden answers can be found everywhere even in nature, even in the trees:

> By midday, warmed
> by the piercing sunshine,
>
> trees shed heaps
> of snow from their limbs
>
> as if slipping out
> of padded
> white kimonos,
>
> stand naked
> in the slanting rays
> like antennas,

> ready
> for communication
>
> with meteors

Multiple acts of transfiguration occur here. Snowy tree limbs become arms clad in "white kimonos," which are luminescent in the "slanting rays" of the sun. Such rays stand out starkly in the landscape just as antennas do in a skyline. Chiaroscuro also highlights the delicate balancing act between nature and urbanization. The treatment of light and shadow in imagery is carefully and precisely controlled; the contrast between the two highlights how light falls unevenly and from a particular direction in order to create meaning. Being able to view things in new light or at different angles is crucial to obtaining new perspectives.

The last lines of the poem complicate this narrative further. They suggest that meteors in space can be communicated with by simple antennas. This seems surreally enigmatic at first and isn't the only instance of space imagery in the book. However, subtext imbues such celestial bodies with bleak implications once other poems unveil the grief of post-war Japan. The poet's concern with objects falling from the sky can be directly translated from the impact bombs can have on a national psyche.

Cultural identity is intrinsically tied with personal identity. The concerns of society become her own. Always, she looks deeply into herself when trying to articulate her convictions, beliefs, and the root of her identity:

> what were you doing
> when the Bomb was dropped? I had no idea how to answer –
> then an internal voice began chanting drowsily, 'seed are stars,
> stars are seeds,' like fading thunder...

> *We were just in time for the train across the mainland for the castle town – but rumor had it that the whole town was contaminated by radiation – that a flying saucer... no, a huge fire ball had burst in the air... ever since then the soil itself has been radioactive... no grass has grown, no birds sung, no fish swum in the sparkling clear water...*

Danno's personal connection with her homeland's history is another facet of her being, another way she re-contextualizes her understanding of the world. The more she realizes its horrors, the stronger her own conviction grows as to why nature is precious, why all life is precious.

So when antennas are "ready / for communication / with meteors," the poet seems to have come to a decision about who she is. The book doesn't react aggressively against meteors. Instead, there is a willingness to connect. Her subtextual grief from the wartime destruction of Hiroshima and Nagasaki instead transforms into a yearning for connectivity, communication, and empathy—all the starting points of peace, human relationships, and mutual understanding.

Danno is good at attributing and tying strong emotions to concrete nature imagery. In the face of all the despair the world can wrought, the speaker of one poem realizes the joy in living:

> *While kicking frantically,*
> *my feet felt a rushing spring and I somehow surfaced. To my surprise*
> *I managed to dog-paddle to the other shore. I was happier than I*
> *had ever felt in my young life when, thoroughly spent, I lay on my*
> *stomach on the sun-warmed pebbles...*

This intense near death experience of drowning intensifies and highlights an appreciation for life. Nature feels very welcoming and warm here, as if cradling the speaker with "sun-warmed pebbles."

Once again light is used as a tool to illuminate the dark morasses of uncertainty. She captures the latter's existential confusion succinctly: "Pears resemble avocados only in shape: / I realize I have no idea what on earth I am."

At first she doesn't have any answers and worries she won't find any. But by persisting in the struggle to understand who she really is, the poet comes closer to solidifying the Self. When she says, "I hope the orbit of my thoughts can be traced more precisely / and the geography in my brain explored in more detail," she shows how strongly she identifies with the very human need for self-discovery.

"I felt as if I had crossed a line – an invisible line / drawn along the meandering ups and downs of the Path…"

Accepting that life is beyond any one person's control means to come to terms with yourself and find peace. Rather than passivity, she is instead advocating for the active choice to believe in beauty, stability, and resiliency.

PUBLICATION CREDITS

Lois P. Jones: "One" was previously published in
Cultural Weekly.

Don Share: "On Screaming Your Head Off" from
Wishbone, 2012, Black Sparrow Books

Melissa Studdard: "For Baudelaire" is from
I Ate the Cosmos for Breakfast, 2015,
Saint Julian Press, Inc.

Contributor Notes

Kelli Allen's work has appeared in numerous journals and anthologies in the US and internationally. She is a four-time Pushcart Prize nominee and has won awards for her poetry, prose, and scholarly work. She served as Managing Editor of *Natural Bridge*, is the current Poetry Editor for *The Lindenwood Review*, and holds an MFA from the University of Missouri St. Louis. She is the director of the River Styx Hungry Young Poets Series and founded the Graduate Writers Reading Series for UMSL. She is currently a Professor of Humanities and Creative Writing at Lindenwood University and teaches for The Pierre Laclede Honors College at UMSL. Her chapbook, *Some Animals*, won the 2016 Etchings Press Prize. Her full-length poetry collection, *Otherwise, Soft White Ash*, arrived from John Gosslee Books in 2012 and was nominated for the Pulitzer Prize. www.kelli-allen.com

Maura Alia Badji's poems and essays have appeared in *The Phoenix Soul*, *The Good Men Project*, *Barely South Review*, *Cobalt*, *The Buffalo Times*, and *The Haight Ashbury Literary Journal*, as well as several literary anthologies. She earned her MFA in Creative Writing at the University of WA, Seattle, where she was an Editorial Assistant at *The Seattle Review*. Maura is a member of The Watering Hole, an online community dedicated to poets of color. She blogs about poetry, art, and life at *The Moxie Bee* (http://www.themoxiebee.com .) A NY State native, she lives in Virginia Beach with her son.

Amy Barone's new poetry chapbook, *Kamikaze Dance*, was published by Finishing Line Press, where she was recognized as a finalist in their New Women's Voices Competition of 2014. Her poetry has appeared in *Gradiva*, *Impolite Conversation (UK)*, *Italian Americana*, *Paterson Literary Review*, *Philadelphia Poets*, *The Rutherford Red Wheelbarrow* and *Wild Violet*, among other publications. She spent five years as Italian correspondent for *Women's Wear Daily* and *Advertising Age*. Her first book, *Views from the Driveway*, was published by Foothills Publishing. From 2012-2015, she served as a board member of the Italian American Writers Association and co-hosted their monthly readings. She belongs to PEN America Center and the brevitas online poetry community that celebrates the short poem. A native of Bryn Mawr, PA, Barone lives in New York City.

Susan Berlin's poems have appeared in *Alaska Quarterly, Asheville Poetry Review, Atlanta Review, Cape Cod Poetry Review, Georgetown Review, Harvard Review, Iodine Poetry Review, Mudfish, Naugatuck River Review, Oberon* and *Ploughshares*, among many others. A multiple Pushcart Prize nominee and two-time Finalist for the National Poetry Series, she was awarded 1st Prize in the Galway Kinnell Poetry Contest and has received an International Publication Prize and an International Merit Award from the Atlanta Review. Susan is the author of *The Same Amount of Ink* (Glass Lyre Press, 2016). She lives in Yarmouth Port, MA.

Jan Bottiglieri lives and writes in suburban Chicago. She is a managing editor for the poetry annual *RHINO* and holds an MFA in Poetry from Pacific University. Jan's poems have appeared in *december, Rattle, DIAGRAM, Willow Springs* and elsewhere, and she has led poetry workshops in the Chicago area. She is the author of the chapbook *Where Gravity Pools the Sugar* and the full-length poetry collection *Alloy* (Mayapple Press, 2015.) Visit janbottiglieri.com.

Patricia Clark is Poet-in-Residence and Professor in the Department of Writing at Grand Valley State University. Author of four volumes of poetry, Patricia's latest book is *Sunday Rising*. She has also published chapbooks titled *Wreath for the Red Admiral* and *Given the Trees*. Her work has been featured on *Poetry Daily* and *Verse Daily*, also appearing in *The Atlantic, Gettysburg Review, Poetry, Slate*, and *Stand*. Recent work appears (or is forthcoming) in *Kenyon Review, New England Review, Southern Humanities Review, North American Review, Plume, Prairie Schooner, Superstition Review*, and elsewhere. Patricia was poet laureate of Grand Rapids from 2005-2007.

Joan Colby has published widely in journals such as *Poetry, Atlanta Review, South Dakota Review*, etc. Awards include two Illinois Arts Council Literary Awards, an Illinois Arts Council Fellowship in Literature. She has published 16 books including *Selected Poems* from FutureCycle Press which received the 2013 FutureCycle Prize and *Ribcage* from Glass Lyre Press which has been awarded the 2015 Kithara Book Prize. She has two books forthcoming in 2016 and 2017. One of her poems is among the winners of the 2016 *Atlantic Review*

International Poetry Contest. Colby is also a senior editor of FutureCycle Press and an associate editor of *Kentucky Review*.

Beth Copeland's second book *Transcendental Telemarketer* (BlazeVOX books, 2012) received the runner up award in the North Carolina Poetry Council's 2013 Oscar Arnold Young Award for best poetry book by a North Carolina writer. Her first book, *Traveling through Glass*, received the 1999 Bright Hill Press Poetry Book Award. Her poems have been published in numerous literary magazines and anthologies, including *The Atlanta Review, New Millennium Writings, The North American Review, Pirene's Fountain, Poet's Market, Rattle, The Southern Poetry Anthology, Tar River Poetry,* and *The Wide Shore: A Journal of Global Women's Poetry*. She has been profiled as poet of the week on the *PBS NewsHour* web site. An assistant professor of English at Methodist University, she lives with her husband in a log cabin in rural North Carolina.

Krista Cox is a paralegal and an associate poetry editor at *Stirring: A Literary Collection*. Her poetry has appeared or is forthcoming in *Rogue Agent, Whale Road Review*, and *Pittsburgh Poetry Review,* among other places. Find her work and more about her at kristacox.me.

Ken Craft is a writer and teacher living west of Boston. His poems have appeared in *Gray's Sporting Journal, Off the Coast, Slant, Angle Journal of Poetry,* and many other journals and e-zines. His debut poetry collection, *The Indifferent World,* was published by Future Cycle Press in April of 2016.

Ivan de Monbrison is a French poet, writer and artist who lives in Paris and Marseille. His poems and short stories have appeared in several literary magazines in France, Italy, Belgium, The UK, Canada, Australia, Switzerland and in the US. Five poetry chapbooks of his works have been published: *L'ombre déchirée, Journal, La corde à nu, Ossuaire* and *Sur-Faces*. His first poem-novel *les Maldormants* has been published in 2014, in France.

Hannah Dellabella is pursuing her MFA in poetry at Purdue University. She is an alumna of Carnegie Mellon, where she studied creative writing and professional writing. She is a native of Bayonne, New Jersey, and is very aware of her Jersey accent. She is a compulsive imaginer.

Lori Desrosiers' poetry books are *The Philosopher's Daughter* (Salmon Poetry, 2013), a chapbook, *Inner Sky* (Glass Lyre Press 2015) and *Sometimes I Hear the Clock Speak* (Salmon Poetry, 2016). Her work has been nominated for a Pushcart Prize. She edits *Naugatuck River Review*, a journal of narrative poetry. She teaches Literature and Composition at Westfield State University and

Holyoke Community College, and Poetry in the Interdisciplinary Studies program for the Lesley University M.F.A. graduate program.

Anthony DiMatteo's work has been spotted roaming recent pages in *The Cortland Review, Smartish Pace, Tar River Review,* and *Verse Daily.* His current book is *In Defense of Puppets* (Future Cycle Press 2016).

Timothy B. Dodd is from Mink Shoals, WV. His poetry has appeared in *The Roanoke Review, Ellipsis, Broad River Review, William & Mary Review, Crannog,* and elsewhere. He is currently in the MFA program at the University of Texas El Paso.

Alexis Rhone Fancher is the author of *How I Lost My Virginity To Michael Cohen and other heart stab poems,* (Sybaritic Press, 2014) and *State of Grace: The Joshua Elegies,* (KYSO Flash Press, 2015). Find her poems in *Rattle, The MacGuffin, Slipstream, Fjords, H_NGM_N, Broadzine, HOBART, Ragazine, Chiron Review, Wide Awake: Poets of Los Angeles, Quaint Magazine, Blotterature, Menacing Hedge,* and elsewhere. Since 2013 she's been nominated for four Pushcart Prizes and four Best of The Net awards. Alexis is poetry editor of *Cultural Weekly,* where she also publishes "The Poet's Eye," a monthly photo essay about her ongoing love affair with Los Angeles. www.alexisrhonefancher.com

Marcene Gandolfo's work has been published widely in journals, including *Bellingham Review, Fifth Wednesday Journal, Poet Lore,* and *DMQ Review.* Last year, her debut book, *Angles of Departure,* won Foreword Reviews' Silver Book of the Year Award. And most recently, she has joined the book review team at *Mom Egg Review.*

Gail Fishman Gerwin (www.gailfgerwin.com) is the author of three poetry collections: *Sugar and Sand* (Paterson Poetry Prize finalist) *Dear Kinfolk* (Paterson Award for Literary Excellence), and *Crowns,* (Aldrich Press, 2016). Her poem "A State in Mind" was a third-prize winner in the 2015 Allen Ginsberg Poetry Awards. She is associate poetry editor of *Tiferet Journal* and is a writing-workshop facilitator. Gail's poetry, book reviews, fiction, essays, and plays appear in print and online journals, in other media, and on stage.

Timothy Green was born in Western New York in 1980. A Rush Rhees and Take Five Scholar at the University of Rochester, Green studied English, biochemistry, psychology, and eastern philosophy, and worked as a technician in a molecular biology lab, supporting research on mRNA binding structures.

He graduated magna cum laude in 2003, earning awards from Phi Beta Kappa, the Golden Key National Honors Society, and the Academy of American Poets.

For two years Green remained in Rochester, working as a group home counselor for adults with schizophrenia.

In 2004, he moved to Southern California to become assistant editor and then editor of *Rattle,* now one of the widest-circulating poetry magazines in the world.

American Fractal, Timothy Green's first book-length collection of poetry, was published by Red Hen Press in 2009. His poems and short stories have appeared in dozens of publications, including The Connecticut Review, Florida Review, Fugue, Gargoyle, Los Angeles Review, Mid-American Review, Nimrod International Journal, Paterson Literary Review, and Runes. An earlier version of American Fractal won the Phi Kappa Phi Student Recognition Award from the University of Southern California, from which he graduated with a Masters in Professional Writing in 2009.

Timothy Green is also co-founder of the annual Wrightwood Literary Festival, and a contributing columnist for the *Press-Enterprise* newspaper. He lives in the mountains near Los Angeles with his wife, Megan Green, and their two children.

Melinda B Hipple's poems and short stories have appeared in numerous print and online publications such as *Encore, Watershed, Hillock, Prune Juice, Tinywords* and *Lynx,* and she has been a regular contributor to *Pirene's Fountain.* Three of her poems were anthologized in *First Water: Best of Pirene's Fountain.* She was a past editor and columnist for Up the Creek News, and haiga editor for two Japanese short form poetry journals—*Notes from the Gean* and *A Hundred Gourds.* In 2016, she was editor of the annual literary magazine *Watershed.*

In addition to poetry, Melinda writes short fiction, creative non-fiction, and mystery and science-fiction novels. Her non-fiction piece "The Cellar" was the first-place winner of the 2014 Moorman Prize for Prose. Her artwork graces the covers of *Floodwater* by Connie Post, and *Ribcage* by Joan Colby.

Lois P. Jones is a recipient of the 2016 Bristol Poetry Prize and the 2012 Tiferet Poetry Prize and was shortlisted for the 2016 Bridport Prize in poetry. Her poetry has been published in anthologies including *The Poet's Quest for God* (Eyewear Publishing), *Wide Awake: Poetry of Los Angeles and Beyond* (The Pacific Coast Poetry Series), *30 Days* (Tupelo Press) and *Good-Bye Mexico* (Texas

Review Press). She has work published or forthcoming in *Tinderbox Poetry Journal, Narrative, American Poetry Journal, Tupelo Quarterly, The Warwick Review, Cider Press Review* and others. She is Poetry Editor of *Kyoto Journal*, host of KPFK's *Poets Café* (Pacifica Radio) and co-hosts Moonday Poetry. Her first poetry collection, *Night Ladder* was released recently from Glass Lyre Press.

Allison Joseph lives, writes, and teaches in Carbondale, Illinois, where she is part of the creative writing faculty at Southern Illinois University. She serves as editor and poetry editor of *Crab Orchard Review*, moderator of the Creative Writers Opportunities List, and director of Writers In Common, a summer writers conference for writers of all ages.

Kateema Lee is a Washington D. C. native. Her poetry has appeared or is forthcoming in print and online journals such as *PMS: Poemmemoirstory, African American Review, Gargoyle, Word Riot* and others, and she is the author of the chapbook, *Almost Invisible* (Kelsay Books, 2016). She is a *Cave Canem* Graduate Fellow, and she attended the Callaloo Workshop at Brown University. When she's not writing, she teaches English and women's studies.

Dennis Maloney is a poet and translator. A number of volumes of his own poetry have been published including *The Map Is Not the Territory: Poems & Translations* and *Just Enough*. His book *Listening to Tao Yuan Ming* was recently published by Glass Lyre Press. His works of translation include: *The Stones of Chile* by Pablo Neruda, *The Landscape of Castile* by Antonio Machado, *Between the Floating Mist: Poems of Ryokan*, and the *The Poet and the Sea* by Juan Ramon Jimenez. He is also the editor and publisher of the widely respected White Pine Press in Buffalo, NY. and divides his time between Buffalo, NY and Big Sur, CA.

John C. Mannone, three-time Pushcart nominee, has over 500 works in venues such as *Inscape Literary Journal, Acentos Review, Windhover, Artemis, Still* and *Town Creek Poetry*. A Tennessean with two literary poetry collections, he edits poetry for *Silver Blade* and *Abyss & Apex*. He's a college professor of physics. Visit http://jcmannone.wordpress.com

Megan Merchant lives in the tall pines of Prescott, AZ. She is the author of two full-length poetry collections: *Gravel Ghosts* (Glass Lyre Press, 2016), *The Dark's Humming* (2015 Lyrebird Award Winner, Glass Lyre Press, 2017), four chapbooks, and a forthcoming children's book with Philomel Books. She was awarded the 2016-2017 COG Literary Award, judged by Juan Felipe Herrera, the Poet Laureate of the United States. You can find her work at meganmerchant.wix.com/poet.

Amy Miller's poetry has appeared in *Bellingham Review, Nimrod, Rattle, Willow Springs,* and *ZYZZYVA*. She won the Cultural Center of Cape Cod National Poetry Competition, judged by Tony Hoagland, and has been a finalist for the Pablo Neruda Prize and the 49th Parallel Award. Recent chapbooks are *Rough House* (White Knuckle Press) and *I Am on a River and Cannot Answer* (BOAAT Press, forthcoming). She works as the publications manager for the Oregon Shakespeare Festival and blogs at writers-island.blogspot.com.

Pamela Miller is a Chicago writer who has published four books of poetry, most recently *Miss Unthinkable* (Mayapple Press, 2013). Her work has recently appeared, or is forthcoming, in *RHINO, Blue Fifth Review, Olentangy Review, New Poetry from the Midwest 2016, After Hours, Caravel, Circe's Lament: Anthology of Wild Women Poetry* and elsewhere.

Hallie Moore, raised in Washington State and educated in California (Stanford University, BS, MA; Antioch University Los Angeles, MFA), now calls the Texas Gulf Coast home. Most recently she is the winner of the 2013 Blue Light Press Chapbook Contest. Her poetry is currently on display in Houston on an 84 foot photo wall on Main Street . Other work has appeared in *The Texas Review, Borderlands, Spillway, Blue Mesa Review, Calyx, Moondance, The Adirondack Review, Suddenly, Persimmon Tree* etc with work forthcoming in *Sugar Mule* and *Black Heart Magazine*.

Cameron Morse taught and studied in China. He is currently an MFA candidate at UMKC and lives with his wife, Lili, in Blue Springs, Missouri. His work has been or will be published in *I-70 Review, TYPO, Otis Nebula, Sleet, Steam Ticket, Referential Magazine, Rufous Review, Small Print Magazine, Two Hawks Quarterly, First Class Literary Magazine* and *District Lit*.

Dipika Mukherjee's two poetry collections include *The Third Glass of Wine* (Kolkata: Writer's Workshop, 2015), and a chapbook, *The Palimpsest of Exile* (Canada: Rubicon Press, 2009). Her debut novel was long-listed for the Man Asian Literary Prize and published as *Thunder Demons* (Gyaana,2011) and republished as *Ode to Broken Things* (Repeater, 2016). Her second novel, *Shambala Junction,* won the Virginia Prize for Fiction (Aurora Metro, 2016). Her short story collections include *Rules of Desire* (Fixi, Malaysia, 2015) and edited collections include *Champion Fellas* (Word Works, 2016), *Silverfish New Writing*

6 (Silverfish, 2006) and *The Merlion and Hibiscus* (Penguin, 2002). She won the Liakoura Prize for Poetry (USA, 2016) and the Gayatri GaMarsh Award for Literary Excellence (USA, 2015) as well as the Platform Flash Fiction Prize (India, 2009). She is Contributing Editor for *Jaggery* and lives in Chicago.

James B. Nicola has had work appear twice previously in *Pirene's Fountain*, w3rdc and recently in the Southwest and Atlanta Reviews, Rattle, and Poetry East. His nonfiction book Playing the Audience won a Choice award. His first full-length poetry collection, Manhattan Plaza, is currently available; his second, Stage to Page: Poems from the Theater, will be out in 2016. A Yale graduate, James has been giving both theater and poetry workshops at libraries, literary festivals, schools, and community centers all over the country. More at sites.google.com/site/jamesbnicola.

Cristina M. R. Norcross is the author of 7 poetry collections. Her most recent books include *Amnesia and Awakenings* (Local Gems Press, 2016), and *Still Life Stories* (Aldrich Press, forthcoming/2016). Her works appear in print and online in North American and international journals, such as *The Toronto Quarterly, Your Daily Poem, Lime Hawk, The Poetry Storehouse, The Avocet,* and *Right Hand Pointing,* among others. Cristina's work also appears in numerous print anthologies. She was a semi-finalist in the 2015 Concrete Wolf Chapbook Competition and a finalist in the 2015 Five Oaks Press Chapbook Contest. Cristina is the founding editor of the online poetry journal, *Blue Heron Review.* She is the co-founder of Random Acts of Poetry and Art Day and a contributing artist to The Art Ambush Project. Find out more about this poet at: www.cristinanorcross.com

Simon Perchik is an attorney whose poems have appeared in *Partisan Review, Forge, Poetry, Osiris, The New Yorker* and elsewhere. His most recent collection is *Almost Rain*, published by River Otter Press (2013). For more information, including free e-books, his essay titled "Magic, Illusion and Other Realities" please visit his website at www.simonperchik.com.

Connie Post served as Poet Laureate of Livermore, California (2005 to 2009). Her work has appeared in *Calyx, Comstock Review, Slipstream, Spoon River Poetry Review, Valparaiso Poetry Review* and Verse Daily. *Her first full length book,* Floodwater *(Glass Lyre Press 2014) won the Lyrebird Award. She is the* winner of the 2016 Crab Creek Review *Poetry Award and won first prize in the 2017 Prick of the Spindle Open Poetry Competition.*

Marcia J. Pradzinski, an award-winning poet, lives in Skokie, Illinois. Her poetry has appeared in print journals, anthologies, and online. Her most recent publications have been in *RHINO* 2015, the Winter and Summer 2016 issues of *Blue Heron Review, The Chronicles of Eve* anthology of *Paper Swans Press, UK,* and *The Ekphrastic Review.* Another poem is forthcoming in *Haibun Today.* Her first chapbook of poems, *Left Behind,* was published by Finishing Line Press in December, 2015.

Sandra Rokoff-Lizut, retired educator and children's book author (published by Macmillan, Holt Reinhart & Winston, and Hallmark Inc.), is currently both a printmaker and poet. She is a member of Oregon Poetry Association and 1st place award winner in their Spring 2014 contest, Mary's Peak Poets, Poetic License, Gertrude's, and a weekly writing salon. Rokoff-Lizut volunteered by teaching poetry to middle-schoolers, at the Boys and Girls Club in Corvallis, She also studied poetry through OSU as well as at Sitka and Centrum. Previous publications include *Illya's Honey, The Bicycle Review, Wilderness House Review, The Penwood Review, Wild Goose Poetry Review* and *Verseweavers.*

M. C. Rush currently resides in upstate New York, has work forthcoming in *Thin Air Magazine,* and has most recently published poems in *Two Thirds North, The Tulane Review, Broad River Review,* and *Whiskey Island.*

Don Share is the editor of *Poetry* magazine. His most recent books are *Wishbone* (Black Sparrow), *Union* (Eyewear), and *Bunting's Persia* (Flood Editions); he has also edited a critical edition of Basil Bunting's poems published by Faber and Faber, a Times (London), and New Statesman, Book of the Year. He is also editing a selection of Bunting's prose. His translations of Miguel Hernández, awarded the Times Literary Supplement Translation Prize and Premio Valle Inclán, were published in a revised and expanded edition by New York Review Books, and also appear in an earlier edition from Bloodaxe Books. His other books include *Seneca in English* (Penguin Classics), *Squandermania* (Salt), and *The Open Door: 100 Poems, 100 Years of POETRY Magazine* (University of Chicago Press), co-edited with Christian Wiman, a sequel to which, *Who Reads Poetry,* will appear this year. His work at *Poetry* has been recognized with three National Magazine Awards for editorial excellence from the American Society of Magazine Editors, and a CLMP (Community of Literary Magazines and Presses) "Firecracker" Award for Best Poetry Magazine. He received a VIDA

"VIDO" Award in 2015 for his "contributions to American literature and literary community."

Susan Sheppard is a native West Virginian of mixed heritage (Delaware, Shawnee and western European). She is the author of a number of books and also oracles, such as *The Phoenix Cards* and the *Black Moon Astrology Cards*. Her work has appeared in a number of magazines over the years such as *Ohio Review, River Styx, Earth's Daughter's, 5 AM* and many others. Sheppard's poetry chapbook *Balefire* was brought out by Crisis Chronicles in 2015. She has owned and operated her own ghost tour in Parkersburg, West Virginia for the past 21 years. Sheppard is also an artist and a doll maker. Sheppard bought her first computer when she won a poetry fellowship in the mid 1990s from the West Virginia Department of Culture & History.

Alison Stone is the author of five poetry collections, including *Ordinary Magic* (NYQ Books, 2016), *Dangerous Enough* (Presa Press 2014), and *They Sing at Midnight*, which won the 2003 Many Mountains Moving Poetry Award and was published by Many Mountains Moving Press. Her poems have appeared in *The Paris Review, Poetry, Ploughshares, Barrow Street, Poet Lore,* and a variety of other journals and anthologies. She has been awarded *Poetry's* Frederick Bock Prize and *New York Quarterly's* Madeline Sadin award. She is also a painter and the creator of The Stone Tarot. A licensed psychotherapist, she has private practices in NYC and Nyack. She is currently editing an anthology of poems on the Persephone/Demeter myth.

Melissa Studdard's books include the poetry collection *I Ate the Cosmos for Breakfast* and the novel *Six Weeks to Yehidah*. Her writings have appeared in a wide range of publications, such as *Poets & Writers, Southern Humanities Review, Harvard Review, The Guardian,* and *Psychology Today*. Her awards include the Forward National Literature Award, the International Book Award, the Kathak Literary Award, the Poiesis Award of Honor International, the Readers' Favorite Award, and two Pinnacle Book Achievement Awards. She is the executive producer and host of

VIDA Voices & Views for VIDA: Women in Literary Arts and an editor for *American Microreviews and Interviews.*

J. Tarwood has been a dishwasher, a community organizer, a medical archivist, a documentary film producer, an oral historian, and a teacher. Much of his life has been spent in East Africa, Latin America, and the Middle East. He has published three books, *And For The Mouth A Flower, Grand Detour* and *The Cats In Zanzibar,* and his poems have appeared in magazines ranging from *American Poetry Review* to *Visions.* He has always been an unlikely man in unlikely places.

Susan Tepper is a twenty year writer and the author of six published books of fiction and poetry. Her seventh book, a novella, will be out later this year from Rain Mountain Press, NYC. Tepper has received numerous awards and honors that include multiple Pushcart nominations and a Pulitzer nomination for the novel. She lives in the NY area with her husband and her dog Otis. www.susantepper.com

Maria Terrone is the author of the poetry collections *Eye to Eye* (Bordighera Press); *A Secret Room in Fall* (McGovern Prize, Ashland Poetry Press) and *The Bodies We Were Loaned* (The Word Works), and a chapbook, *American Gothic, Take 2.* Her work, which has been published in French and Farsi and nominated four times for a Pushcart Prize, has appeared in magazines including *Poetry, Ploughshares* and *The Hudson Review* and in more than 25 anthologies. She is also the poetry editor of the journal *Italian Americana.*

Caitlin Thomson has an MFA from Sarah Lawrence College. Her poems have been nominated for the Pushcart Prize and the Best of the Net Anthology. *Territory Prayer,* her third chapbook was just published by Maverick Duck Press. You can learn more about her writing at www.caitlinthomson.com.

Wren Tuatha's poems have appeared in *The Baltimore Review, The Loch Raven Review, Digges' Choice, The Baltimore Women's Times, The Green Revolution* and the anthology *Blood and Tears.* She received a Young Authors Award in Poetry from *The Courier Journal.* Her poetry-based stage play, *This Is How She Steps on Snakes,* was funded by grants from

Towson University's Women's Center and Office of Diversity. The journal *Grub Street* awarded her first prize for slam poetry. She currently lives in a log cabin on a California mountain with her partner, activist and author C.T. Lawrence Butler. They are often followed by goats or chasing their sheltie, Cricket, who feels the true way to save the world is to herd all its squirrels into manageable affinity groups.

Political activist and wilderness advocate, **Pam Uschuk** has howled out six books of poems, including *Crazy Love,* winner of a 2010 American Book Award and her most recent, *Blood Flower* (2015, Wings Press). Translated into more than a dozen languages, Uschuk's many awards include the New Millenium Poetry Prize, 2010 Best of the Web, the Struga International Poetry Prize (for a theme poem), the Dorothy Daniels Writing Award from the National League of American PEN Women. Uschuk edited the anthology, *Truth To Power: Writers Respond To The Rhetoric Of Hate And Fear,* and she's finishing on a multi-genre book called *The Book Of Healers Healing; An Odyssey Through Ovarian Cancer.*

Ann Wehrman's poetry, short fiction, literary analysis, and creative non-fiction have appeared in various publications including *Poetry Now, Convergence, Blue Heron Review, Tule Review, Medusa's Kitchen, WTF, The Ophidian, Rattlesnake Review, Calaveras Station Literary Journal, Cosumnes River Journal,* and *Sacramento News & Review.* Her 2007 broadside, *Notes from the Ivory Tower,* and her 2011 self-illustrated chapbook, *Inside (love poems),* are available from Rattlesnake Press. Ann can be found teaching English composition online, playing classical flute, and practicing/teaching yoga. She currently lives in Sacramento, CA.

Martin Willitts Jr is a retired Librarian. He won the 2014 Dylan Thomas International Poetry Contest; *Rattle* Ekphrastic Challenge, June 2015, Editor's Choice; *Rattle* Ekphrastic Challenge, Artist's Choice, November 2016. He has over 20 chapbooks including the *Turtle Island Quarterly* Editor's Choice Award, *The Wire Fence Holding Back the World* (Flowstone Press). He has 11 full-length collections including *How to Be Silent*

(FutureCycle Press, 2016) and *Dylan Thomas and the Writing Shed* (FutureCycle Press, 2017).

Jane Yolen, often called "the Hans Christian Andersen of America," is the author of over 366 books. Her work has won numerous awards--two Nebulas, a World Fantasy Award, a Caldecott Medal, three Golden Kite awards, three Mythopoeic awards, two Christopher Medals, a nomination for the National Book Award, and the Jewish Book Award, among others. Six colleges and universities have given her honorary doctorates. She is a GrandMaster three times: for Science Fiction/Fantasy Writers of America (SFWA), Science Fiction Poetery Association (SFPA), and the World Fantasy Association. She's been on the board of the Society of Children's Book Writers and Illustrators for the past 45 years.(SCBWI). Also worthy of note, her Skylark Award--given by NESFA, the New England Science Fiction Association, set her good coat on fire. Visit www.janeyolen.com

The Crafty Poet II
A Portable Workshop

edited by

Diane Lockward

Companion volume to the original *The Crafty Poet: A Portable Workshop.*

Poetry tutorial ideal for use in the classroom, in workshops, or at home. Craft tips, model poems, and prompts. Includes more than 100 of our finest poets such as Tony Hoagland, Laura Kasischke, Alberto Rios, and Ellen Bass.

Terrapin Books
www.terrapinbooks.com
ISBN: 978-0996987172
$21.99 / 327 pages
Available from Amazon, B&N, and wherever books are sold

The Aeolian Harp Series, Volume 3

GUEST EDITOR
JON TRIBBLE OF CRAB ORCHARD REVIEW

Featuring
Devon Balwit
Ruth Goring
Peter Goodwin
Lana Bella
Andrena Zawinski
Lois Marie Harrod
Petra Kuppers
Karen Schubert
Marc Frazier
Hedy Habra

Available Winter 2017!

MENTOR FOR POETS

Work one on one with an experienced poet and editor who will target your concerns and provide comprehensive feedback as well as customized prompts to support the continued growth of your work. By editing for thousands of writers, I've honed my ability to tune into an individual's voice as well as clarify, strengthen and extend its signal. As a mentor, I apply these skills to identify the most authentic, descriptive, expressive and original passages of each draft and help poets build outward from there. Feedback for advanced writers also includes scansion and color-coded analysis of the immanent music in your drafts, along with suggestions for developing those motifs further. Links to relevant poems, theory and visual art are integrated into each response. With an MFA in Poetry from Syracuse University, an MFA in Sculpture from NY Academy of Art, and a BA in English from Harvard, I'm eager to share what I've learned. Winner of the National Poetry Contest (UK) and The Ledge Poetry Prize. Assistant Poetry Editor at *The Cortland Review*. Invest in your growth as a writer: $40 per poem, $150 for a group of four. Reach me at ericberlin@me.com. I look forward to helping!

Glass Lyre Press

exceptional works to replenish the spirit

Glass Lyre Press is an independent literary publisher interested in technically accomplished, stylistically distinct, and original work. Glass Lyre seeks diverse writers that possess a dynamic aesthetic and an ability to emotionally and intellectually engage a wide audience of readers.

Glass Lyre's vision is to connect the world through language and art. We hope to expand the scope of poetry and short fiction for the general reader through exceptionally well-written books, which evoke emotion, provide insight, and resonate with the human spirit.

Poetry Collections
Poetry Chapbooks
Select Short & Flash Fiction
Anthologies

www.GlassLyrePress.com

www.ingramcontent.com/pod-product-compliance
Lightning Source LLC
Chambersburg PA
CBHW021437080526
44588CB00009B/562